A FEVER AT THE CORE

JEFFREY MEYERS

A FEVER
AT THE CORE

The Idealist in Politics

*

BARNES & NOBLE
BOOKS
10 East 53d St., New York 10022
(a division of Harper & Row Publishers, Inc.)

© Jeffrey Meyers 1976

Published in the U.S.A. 1976 by
Harper & Row Publishers, Inc.
Barnes & Noble Import Division

ISBN 0 06 494791 2
LC 75 43049

Designed and printed in England by
The Compton Press Ltd, The Old Brewery
Tisbury, Wiltshire

CONTENTS

To Phillip and Yvonne

INTRODUCTION

There is a fire
And motion of the soul which will not dwell
In its own narrow being, but aspire
Beyond the fitting medium of desire;
And, but once kindled, quenchless evermore,
Preys upon high adventure, nor can tire
Of aught but rest; a fever at the core,
Fatal to him who bears, to all who ever bore.

BYRON, *Childe Harold's Pilgrimage*

A man in his own secret meditation,
Is lost amid the labyrinth that he has made,
In art or politics.

YEATS, *1919*

Byron's adventure in Greece, especially his conflict between egoism and idealism, provides a paradigm of the romantic temperament in politics. Byron first travelled in Greece during 1809–1810, and the first two cantos of *Childe Harold's Pilgrimage,* published two years later, reflected his exotic experience as well as his philhellenic sentiments:

Fair Greece! sad relic of departed worth!
Immortal, though no more; though fallen, great!
Who now shall lead thy scattered children forth,
And long accustomed bondage uncreate?

Though these libertarian ideas did not originate with Byron, he was the first to express them in a best-seller; and the international influence of his character and works drew serious attention to the plight of the Greeks struggling against Turkish domination and transformed the philhellenic movement into the great romantic crusade of the post-Napoleonic era. When the Greek Revolution broke out in the spring of 1821 the educated public believed that the battle against the Turks would "regenerate" the modern Greeks and restore their former glories, for as Byron wrote in *The Siege of Corinth* (1816):

> Despite of every yoke she bears,
> That land is glory's still and theirs.

Byron was elected to the Greek revolutionary committee and connected the two worlds of London and Greece. To the English Radicals he lent the prestige of his noble birth; to the philhellenes he was an inspiring leader; to the Greeks a hero and a Messiah. Byron, who had some abortive revolutionary experience with the Carbonari in Italy, reached Missolonghi in January 1824. The Greeks of that marshy and miasmic town had massacred the Turks in 1821; withstood a siege in 1822; welcomed Byron in 1824; surrendered to Turkish forces in 1826; and recaptured the town in 1829 at the end of the war.

At the time of Byron's arrival the Greeks were torn by factionalism, intrigue and self-interest, and he observed: "They seem to have no enemies in heaven or on earth to be dreaded but their own tendency to discord among themselves." Byron spent his three months in Missolonghi attempting to reconcile the Greek leaders, organize his private army of Albanian brigands, plan an assault on the fortress of Lepanto, and arrange for officers, arms and money to be sent from England. He failed in all these objectives, was plagued by earthquakes and epilepsy, mutiny and murder, and lamented to Count Gamba: "I begin to fear that I have done nothing but lose time, money, patience and health" and have met only "with deception, and calumney, and ingratitude". One month before his death he observed that "My situation here is unbearable. A town without any resources, and a government without money; imprisoned by the floods, unable to take any exercise, pestered by demands, without the means of satisfying them or doing anything to relieve them, or myself." As Harold Nicolson remarks, "He had lost his health, his reputation, even his honour."

But Byron's exemplary and sacrificial death did more for the Greek cause than he had ever done while alive. It inspired a flood of books, drew attention to the desperate situation in Greece and seemed to lend respectability to patriotic revolutions. Six days after his death an English ship brought the first part of the Greek loan, and returned with his body. And five years later the concerted intervention of foreign powers achieved what the Greeks themselves had never been able to do, for the combined fleets of England, France and Russia destroyed the Turkish navy at Navarino and secured the liberation of Greece.

Byron's union of thought and action, art and politics; his political idealism and fight for the abstract concept of liberty rather than for the specific cause; his realization of egoistic fantasies, flamboyant costume and theatrical behaviour; his need to escape boredom and quest for danger, excitement and adventures; his passionate desire to change the world by his own idiosyncratic effort; his ambition to achieve military glory by fulfilling the destiny of a nation; his glorious failure, his self-sacrifice and his death-wish ("Seek out—less often sought than found,/A soldier's grave—for thee the best")—all these qualities represent an almost irresistible model for the romantic idealists, who seem to comprise a synthesis of Byronic characteristics. Wilfred Blunt, who married Byron's granddaughter, had his handsome looks and amorous success; Cunninghame Graham had his aristocratic Scottish birth and his refined dandyism; Gabriele D'Annunzio, who saw himself as a Latin Byron, steeped in sensuality and violence, had the same theatrical narcissism and also used politics as a stage for his operatic life. T. E. Lawrence had Byron's courage and his fame, André Malraux his sophistication and style, and Roger Casement his sacrificial death. Like Byron, these romantic idealists exemplified the outsider as charismatic national leader : Blunt, Graham and Casement (an Ulster Protestant) with the Irish, D'Annunzio with the Italians of the Austrian Empire, Lawrence with the Arabs, Malraux with the Spaniards. And, like Byron, they all maintained an aristocratic superiority to their (frequently devoted) followers and used their nationalistic crusades to encourage radical movements—Home Rule, Socialism, anti-Imperialism —in their own country.

In *Fallen Oaks* Malraux quotes Nietzsche's observation that since 1860 nihilism has gradually overtaken all artists and suggests that most of the genius from Baudelaire to our time has been nihilistic. *A Fever at the Core* concerns six men who opposed this nihilistic tradition and were politically active in the fifty years between 1887 and 1937. Wilfred Blunt, Cunninghame Graham, Roger Casement, Gabriele D'Annunzio, T. E. Lawrence and André Malraux were by nature reflective and imaginative, they did not channel their energy solely into literature, but became political leaders and expressed their ideas through action.

They believed, with Lawrence, that the individual is important "if he pushes the right way . . . Only a few men had honestly tried to be greater than mankind : and only their strainings and wrestlings really fill my stomach." Conrad told Graham, "You're a Hamlet choosing to be a Quixote," and all these men were Hamlet types who—in what Erik Erikson calls "The Event," the synthesis, culmination and turning point of a lifetime's experience—yielded to the quixotic impulse and propelled themselves into political life with disastrous or tragic results.

Blunt, Graham and Casement were deeply involved in the struggle for Home Rule. Blunt's event came during the land war in Ireland in 1887; his friend Graham's moment was in the Battle of Trafalgar Square in the same year; and Casement, who sought Blunt's advice about Irish affairs, sacrificed himself when he landed on the coast of Ireland in 1916 to join the Easter rising. Both Blunt and Lawrence actively fought for Arab independence. The former predicted the rise of Arab nationalism that was first manifest in the Mahdi, and the latter sparked this nascent nationalism into the Arab Revolt and achieved his goal in the capture of Damascus in 1918. As Lawrence, who once planned to write Casement's biography, argued the Arab cause before the Great Powers at the Paris Peace Conference, D'Annunzio defied these Powers when he captured Fiume in 1919 and held the city for sixteen months. The mythomania and romantic individualism of D'Annunzio and Lawrence culminated in Malraux, who was profoundly influenced by Lawrence and whose crucial moment came when he led the Escadre España in the Spanish Civil War in 1936.

"All men dream : but not equally," writes Lawrence. "The dreamers of the day are dangerous men, for they may act their dreams with open eyes, to make them possible." These six men were stimulated to action by their idealistic dreams, but could not come to terms with political reality. They all were out of sympathy with contemporary life and looked to the more romantic traditions of an earlier age for their ideals : Blunt with the Bedouins, Graham with the gauchos, Casement with the Celts of western Ireland, D'Annunzio with the *Risorgimento*, Lawrence with the Crusaders and Malraux with the Spanish peasants. They wanted to disestablish the old world and to create a new one, to make reality correspond to their imagination. But they found that political power is not gained by imagination, but by organization.

These versatile and highly individualistic men were temperamentally unsuited to political life, and their overweening egoism, so necessary to art, led them to flamboyant and narcissistic excesses. Blunt and D'Annunzio were notorious libertines, Casement and Lawrence guilt-ridden homosexuals, and they all projected their sexual attitudes into politics. They made no distinction between personal and political goals, and saw politics as a means to self-realization through individual fulfil-ment. Though their charismatic leadership was impressive, it was ephemeral; and they could not build a political organization nor sustain a serious defeat. They provided oratory, not argument; they were picturesque, not practical; they made the theatrical gesture, not the steady advance. The parabola of their careers inevitably moved from intense vitality, energy and enthusiasm to a brief moment of triumph, and then to bitter disillusionment, withdrawal and renunciation. They all had a fatal attraction to failure—which seemed more aristocratic and redemptive than success—as well as a streak of masochistic self-sacrifice. There was a deep and irrational contradiction between their temperamental activism and their philosophical pessimism.

They all exemplify the problem of the intellectual as a man of action. "For a thinker, the revolution's a tragedy," Malraux writes in *Man's Hope.* "The path that leads from moral standards to political activity is strewn with our dead selves. Always there is the conflict between the man who acts and the conditions of his action." Despite their failure and defeat, there was an impressive inner consistency between their thought and action; between their moral and intellectual beliefs and the application of these values to political life. Like Camus, they believed, "It is not the struggle which makes us into artists, but art which compels us to join in the struggle. By his very calling, the artist stands witness for liberty, and this is a justification for which he can be required to pay dearly. By his very calling, he is involved in the thickest depths of history, at the place where the very flesh of man struggles to find breath."

Politics was tragedy for these six idealists, who were always on the right, that is, the losing side. For Casement and D'Annunzio, who saw history merely as an extension of the self, there was a direct connection between lust and power; and their egoistic desire for self-glorification (like Norman Mailer) and for martyrdom (like Yukio Mishima) ended in chaos and disaster. Though Blunt, Graham and Malraux also failed to effect a political change, their *beau geste* had a clarity of vision and humanitarian involvement that was both noble and inspiring. Only

Lawrence, driven by a demonic will, actually succeeded in achieving his political ambitions and creating what he called a "new Asia," but he destroyed himself in the course of his ironic victory. *A Fever at the Core* suggests that though the sensitive, scrupulous and imaginative idealist is capable of making a creative contribution to political life, he is doomed to failure in modern politics because of his very virtues. These idealists are significant not for what they achieved, but for what they were and what they represented. As Freud writes, "The great man influences his contemporaries in two ways: through his personality and through the idea for which he stands."

J.M.

WILFRED SCAWEN BLUNT

(1840-1922)

I shall go in the direction of the firing.

WILFRED SCAWEN BLUNT

Wilfred Scawen Blunt—poet, lover, man of fashion, diplomat, orientalist, traveller, anti-imperialist, sportsman, host and breeder of Arab horses—an artist by nature and politician by accident, defined himself in terms of contraries whose tensions he never resolved :

> He was a man of ideas opposed to those of his own people and his own generation, who, though his talent was recognized as a writer, failed to find disciples. He was an aristocrat in a democratic age, an orientalist out of harmony with received orientalist ideas, a poet who was never popular, and an artist who was never more than an amateur.

Blunt's long life began early in the Victorian age and ended after the Great War. Though a Tory, fox-hunting, landowning, wealthy aristocrat, "by instinct of birth a conservative to my inmost fibre, a believer in tradition and the value of all that is ancient in our national institutions and creeds and moralities," he involved himself in the struggles for freedom in colonial India and Egypt. His most significant political action, however, took place during the Irish land war in 1887, for in this episode Blunt went dramatically and publicly against the interests of his own class to support the evicted peasants against absentee English landlords. In spite of his genuine compassion for the victims of oppression and his willingness to forgo the esteem of society, Blunt's intellectual idealism and physical courage conflicted with the egoism and pride of his character and class. When events failed to match his ambitious expectations, he became disillusioned, left politics and retired into private life.

Blunt's father, Francis, was a contemporary of Byron at Harrow. He served as an Ensign in the Grenadier Guards under Sir John Moore in the Peninsular War, was permanently lamed in the battle of Corunna and obliged to leave the army. He returned to his four thousand acres of land in Sussex, and became a keen sportsman and High Tory supporter of the Duke of Wellington. Wilfred Blunt was born in 1840, and after the death of his father two years later, his beautiful mother came under the influence of Cardinal Manning and was converted to Catholicism. Her three children were received into the Church in 1852, the year before her death. Blunt, who was educated by tutors in England and on the continent, entered the Jesuit school at Stonyhurst instead of Harrow. Though he lost his faith after a retreat in 1862 and abandoned himself to a life of pleasure, his residual Catholicism emerged in moments of mysticism, and led to a fondness for clerical company and a ready sympathy with the Irish independence movement. Blunt's moral and physical life were closely connected, and he wrote that after a climbing accident in the Alps in 1858 his sudden surge of courage was "a revelation of the possibilities of manly action in the world which never left me afterwards; and I think my physical cowardice thus easily overcome has been in part the reason of what moral courage I have had at my command in later years."

Blunt's early life was marked by social success and freedom from responsibility. He entered the diplomatic service in 1859 and was successively secretary of the legation at Athens, Frankfurt, Madrid in the reign of Queen Isabella, Paris at the time of Napoleon III, Lisbon, Buenos Aires and Berne. He fought a bull in Madrid in 1862 and celebrated that sport in his poem "Sancho Sanchez"; acquired a slave in the Cape Verde Islands and brought him to England in 1867; and the following year in the Argentine met Sir Richard Burton, whose ferocious countenance reminded him of a "black leopard, caged, but unforgiving." Blunt was not burdened with politics in those idle and leisurely days and relates that

I wrote poems, not despatches, and though I assisted diplomatically at some of the serious dramas of the day in Europe, it was in the spirit of a spectator rather than of an actor . . . We attachés and junior secretaries were very clearly given to understand that it was not our business to meddle with the politics of the Courts to which we were accredited, only to make ourselves agreeable socially, and amuse ourselves, decorously, if possible, but at any rate in the reverse of any serious sense. It is no exaggeration when I affirm that in the whole twelve years of my diplomatic life I was asked to discharge no duty of the smallest professional importance.

But the decade of diplomatic experience did provide Blunt with a valuable knowledge of foreign affairs and a personal acquaintance with many leading political figures, and throughout his life Blunt had, paradoxically, powerful connections but no real power.

Blunt was exceptionally handsome, well-born and rich, and had a great many love affairs. In 1863 he began a liaison with Catherine Walters ("Skittles"), one of the most famous courtesans of the late nineteenth century, who inspired his *Songs and Sonnets of Proteus* (1875), *Love Sonnets of Proteus* (1881) and *Esther* (1892); and Blunt later claimed that she had "set his passion so full ablaze that it burnt out once for all." Though Blunt was a poet more by temperament and *sprezzatura* than by vision and achievement, he was pleased that his earliest sonnets "gave me almost at once a certain rank in the literary world which was not altogether without its influence on my subsequent relations with my political friends." His political adventures also stimulated his love life, and when he was released from prison in Ireland he soon found that this episode, far from discrediting him with the ladies, "was a title to romantic interest which made it easy to resume my place and more than my place in [their] society."

Blunt married Byron's wealthy granddaughter, Lady Anne Noel, in 1869, but their love was essentially non-carnal (Frank Harris describes her as "a dried up, crabbed little creature"). Blunt's hedonistic feeling that "Love is of the body, the physical passion of joy," was alien to her more spiritual beliefs; and he saw no inconsistency in expecting absolute loyalty from a wife whom he continually deceived. When Lady Anne converted to Catholicism in 1880, Blunt, who egoistically demanded and received the complete adoration of his wife and only child Judith (who was born in 1873), voiced the extraordinary complaint that she had "destroyed the sense I had up to that time had of security and permanence in the devotion you gave me. I have felt ever since you were, so to say, serving another master, acknowledging another king, worshipping another god." His vanity prevented him from recognizing the absurdity of this remark, and in his marriage as in his later political adventures he wanted to be worshipped as a hero.

Edith Finch writes that Blunt "was fastidious and not exceptionally passionate, but love affairs were part of the social game in which his charm and good looks gave him the advantage . . . They were doubtless known to his own circle and were not regarded as surprising. But after a narrow escape from the charge of co-respondent in a well-known divorce case in 1876 he conducted them with extreme discretion." Blunt's devoted biographers have unfortunately maintained this discretion and the full extent of his sexual adventures must remain obscure until his complete diaries are published. But Emily Lutyens' *A Blessed Girl* provides a titillating account of how the middle-aged poet tried to seduce her when as a teenager she visited his daughter, and Sir Sydney Cockerell (who was Blunt's secretary from 1898 to 1908) quotes one revealing entry from Blunt's diary of 1916:

He said that [his love affairs] had been numerous and that he regretted nothing and that he thought he could say he had added to the happiness of many women, and that he had made no woman lastingly unhappy. Many of those he had loved were dead, but those alive remained his friends. He thought it possible to be in love with three women at the same time.

Though Blunt had no regrets, he was quite wrong about making "no woman lastingly unhappy," for his adultery engendered a profound bitterness in both his wife and his daughter which was to have grave effects at the end of his life.

Blunt retired from the diplomatic service after his marriage; and in 1872 when his older brother died, Blunt carved an impressive mortuary statue, and became the heir of his father's estates at Crabbet Park and Newbuildings. He established his reputation as a love poet in 1875; and two years later he became the host of the fashionable and convivial Crabbet Club, whose aristocratic members included George Curzon and Lord Alfred Douglas and whose object was "to discourage serious views of life by holding up a constant standard of amusement." Blunt's cousin, the poet and diplomat George Wyndham, rather preciously pronounced that the annual "occasion is a man's party, barring the hostess, Lady Anne Blunt: they meet to play lawn tennis [sometimes quite naked], the piano, the fool and other instruments of gaiety. To write *bouts rimés*, sonnets and make sham orations."

In the winters the Blunts travelled in the East. The first visit to Egypt in 1875, and the journeys to the Arabian peninsula in 1877 and 1878, recorded in Lady Anne's *The Bedouin Tribes of the Euphrates* (1879) and *A Pilgrimage to Nejd* (1881), inspired new interests that had a lasting influence on Blunt's life. For as Finch writes :

In the Nejd the Blunts had found the supreme example of a country quite independent, with a government suitable and wholly satisfactory to its people, who though poor were contented . . . In Nejd, as nowhere in Europe, were to be found in actual existence liberty, equality, brotherhood. No taxes, no police, no conscription, no compulsion of any kind fettered and irritated the inhabitants, since their ruler depended on the citizens' good will : his army was made up of citizen soldiery. In short, as Blunt later wrote, this view "of the ancient system of free government existing for so many centuries in the heart of that wonderful peninsula, was to confirm in me the enthusiastic love and admiration I already entertained for the Arabian race." It became to Blunt a symbol of what subject races and nations should work toward.

Though Blunt insisted he was not "one of those who love the East only for its picturesque aspects," the noble and independent life of the Bedouin exerted a strong attraction for him. Blunt idealized their anarchistic existence and dismissed the traditional Victorian justification of imperialism—the progress and civilization which the colonizing power supposedly brought to less advanced races—as "debased industrialism, crude cookery and flavourless religion." He was one of the first men to consider indigenous culture as a serious alternative to colonial rule.

After 1877, when Blunt brought Arab mares to England to form the nucleus of the world-famous Crabbet stud which still exists today, the breeding and racing of thoroughbred horses became one of the dominant interests in his life; and he believed, "If I can introduce a pure Arab breed of horses into England and help to set Arabia free of the Turks, I shall not have quite lived in vain." His commitment to the Arabs was also manifested in his serious study of their language (Blunt and his wife, an expert linguist, translated Arabic poetry into

English) and their religion (he was taught Islamic doctrine at Al-Azhar University in Cairo), as well as in his purchase in 1882 of Sheikh Obeyd. Blunt proudly wrote that this estate on the edge of the desert at Heliopolis, nine miles northwest of Cairo, "was then the best fruit garden in Egypt, enclosed in a wall with a bountiful supply of water, and contained, on estimation, 70,000 fruit trees, all in splendid order."

During his second journey to Arabia in 1879 Blunt was invited by his friend, Lord Lytton, the Viceroy of India, to spend the summer at Simla; and on this brief but revealing visit he first conceived the thought that India was selfishly and unwisely governed. In 1883, after his serious involvement with Colonel Arabi and the Egyptian revolution, Blunt visited the exiled Arabi in Ceylon, and then returned to India for a longer tour of all the major cities and an inquiry into the political and social conditions under imperialism. He was in Calcutta during the fierce controversy about the Ilbert Bill (which proposed that Indian magistrates be allowed to try Englishmen); supported plans to found a Moslem university; successfully interceded with the Viceroy, Lord Ripon, on behalf of Indians seeking reform in Hyderabad; and strenuously defended his Indian friends when they were physically threatened by a Scottish doctor for coming too close to him on a crowded railway platform. Blunt noted that this apparently minor incident "made a prodigious sensation, as it was the first time an Englishman had openly taken part with natives against his fellow countrymen."

In *India Under Ripon* (based on his diaries of 1883) and *Ideas About India* (1885) Blunt proposed certain liberal measures that were considered preposterous at the time but were officially adopted many years later : reforms in taxation, the Civil Service and the Army, the creation of provincial councils and parliaments, and a plan for ultimate self-government that would avert the danger of revolt. His political and social ideas, which evolved from his friendships with Indians, resemble those later expressed by E. M. Forster in *A Passage to India* (1924). Blunt admired the political intelligence of the Indians and "believed the natives capable of governing themselves far better than we can do it, and at about a tenth part of the expense"; questioned "whether any one had calculated the number of miles of macadamized roads in the various Anglo-Indian cantonments, not a yard of which had ever served any purpose beyond that of enabling the officers' wives to pay each other visits in their carriages?"; and blamed the unwillingness of the Englishwoman in India to meet the natives on equal social terms for "half the bitter feelings there between race and race."

Blunt also prophesied with startling accuracy the passive resistance movement that did not take place for another half-century and warned that if Indians did not cooperate with the government "we could not maintain our rule for an hour. As it was, they had only to combine against us passively to make the whole machine stop working . . . Let India be united, as Ireland and Egypt are, in a common hatred for all that is English, and our rule there will *ipso facto* cease." Blunt's books opposed all contemporary ideas about imperialism and gave great offence to government officials who, as he remarked, "cannot understand how I, with my position, of an English gentleman and landowner, can go in for revolution in Egypt and India." But he also recognized the limitations of his revolutionary enthusiasm and acknowledged his failure to do more for the Indian nationalists : "I suppose my mind lacked the impetus of a full faith, without which complete devotion to a cause . . . could not be."

Blunt's considerable experience in Arabia and India led directly to his more profound involvement in the nationalist politics of Egypt and Ireland. At the time of his first visit to Egypt in 1875 Blunt was still "a believer in the common English creed that England had a providential mission in the East, and that our wars were only waged there for honest and beneficent reasons. Nothing was further from my mind than that we English could ever be guilty, as a nation, of a great betrayal of justice in arms for our mere selfish interests." As late as 1879 Blunt, "constitutionally shy in early life, had shrunk from publicity in any shape," and had never even entered the House of Commons, made a speech, written an article or sent a letter to a newspaper. But during his annual winter visits to Egypt in the late 1870s he played an increasingly active role in Egyptian affairs. In 1882, Blunt states, "I registered a vow that I would devote a share of my energies thenceforth to the cause of freedom for the Arab race . . . I looked upon Egypt already like a second *patria,* and intended to throw in my lot with the Egyptians as if they were my own countrymen."

Toward the end of 1881 a conflict broke out between the weak Khedive Tewfik and Colonel Ahmed Arabi. The Khedive was supported by the English government, which had taken control of the chaotic Egyptian Treasury in 1877 in order to protect their interest in the Suez

Canal. The nationalistic colonel, who opposed both foreign control of Egyptian affairs and the domination of the army by Turkish-speaking officers, was backed by the Egyptian masses. As a high-minded, well-informed and sympathetic resident of Egypt, Blunt became the unofficial intermediary between the English administrators and the Arab leaders. He first met Arabi in December 1881 and saw in him a reflection of himself, for Blunt observed that the idealistic and mystical fellah leader "in his dreamy way, followed where his fortune led him, and with an ever-growing suspicious belief in his high-destiny and his providential mission as a saviour of his people." And Blunt managed to invest Arabi, whom an Egyptian historian calls "a simple man, lacking in subtlety and political refinement, but possessing courage and boldness," with a "halo of romance which as champion of the fellah wrongs was certainly his due"—just as Lawrence later idealized Emir Feisal. Blunt helped to make Egyptian complaints public when he drafted a nationalist manifesto and published it in *The Times* of January 3, 1882.

Soon after this proclamation the army forced the Khedive to form a nationalist government with Arabi as Minister of War. The English Foreign Office was advised by their Egyptian Consul-General, Sir Edward Malet, that "we can only regain our ascendency by the destruction of the military supremacy" and that only "a government subservient to the interest of the Powers was a safe one," and began to consider military intervention in Egypt to protect their resident subjects, their substantial investments, their heavy shipping in the Canal and their principal route to India. Blunt came to England in March 1882 to act as a propagandist for the nationalist cause and to prevent the occupation of Egypt; but despite his efforts, the English despatched a fleet to Alexandria in May. The menacing warships intensified the hatred of foreigners, and events reached a crisis in June 1882 when serious riots erupted in Alexandria and about three hundred people, including many Europeans, were killed. The English believed the nationalists had inspired the riots and that the country was in complete chaos; and when in July the nationalists strengthened the fortifications in the harbour of Alexandria, the fleet bombarded the city, which was then abandoned by Arabi's rebellious army and left to the rioting mob.

After conversations with General Garnet Wolseley, Blunt had correctly guessed the English military plan of violating the neutrality of the Canal Zone and attacking Egypt from the east, and had given this information to Arabi. But the English army, which the Khedive called in to quell the rebellion and restore order, landed unopposed in Ismailia and in September defeated the nationalists at Tel-el-Kebir. Arabi surrendered and was tried for treason; and Blunt interceded on his behalf, engaged counsel for the defence, paid £5000 in legal fees, and pleaded for justice and Arabi's life. In the course of the trial the Foreign Office gained an admission of rebellion against the Khedive to justify their armed intervention and, largely due to Blunt's efforts, Arabi and his fellow officers had their sentence of death commuted to exile in Ceylon. Blunt attempted to vindicate their cause in his polemical anti-imperialistic poem, *The Wind and the Whirlwind* (1883). Though Blunt believed that his efforts on behalf of the prisoners was the cause of his exclusion from Egypt for the next three years, it is more likely that this banishment was prompted by the seditious encouragement he gave to the nationalists. For in *The Secret History of the English Occupation of Egypt* he made the extremely damaging admission that he was "in considerable measure responsible for the determination the Nationalists came to to risk their country's fortune on the die of battle."

Despite this political conspiracy, which prompted Lord Houghton's remark, "He knows he has a handsome head and he wants it to be seen on Temple Bar," the Foreign Office looked upon Blunt as a sentimental visionary, "a stormy petrel and wayward apostle of lost causes," and a romantic enthusiast who dreamed idle and impractical dreams of an Arab Utopia. He was considered more an irritant than a serious challenge to those in power. Blunt's own view of the Arabi revolt as recorded in his *Secret History* is gravely suspect, for he was unable to fulfil his aim of writing a "secret" and an objective history at the same time. His historical method is too careless and too casual, he often loses the thread of the historical narrative in the long-winded descriptions of his own machinations, tends to exaggerate his own importance, is enamoured of gossip and violently partisan. Conrad, in an incisive comment on Blunt's *Diaries,* which share the same defects as his histories, noticed the vanity, frivolity, egoism and insincerity that sometimes seeped into Blunt's account of his cross-grained opposition to contemporary society :

It is very curious reading, but somehow one cannot take it very seriously. What surprised me most was to discover how much there is of a mere society man in the writer, who takes himself and his feelings seriously only up to a certain point. A personality in antagonism to its proper sphere is always interesting; but . . . I can't divest myself of the suspicion that all this is merely an attitude and nothing more, or at least very little more. All his indignations may be just, but one asks oneself how much they are justified in that particular individual.

Though Blunt had given misguided encouragement to the Egyptians, he still had a great following among the Arabs because of his successful defence of Arabi. And during the Sudan War of 1885 the British government seriously thought of sending Blunt to make peace with the fanatical Mahdi, who had come to prominence during the Egyptian crisis of 1881 and had defeated the equally fanatical General Gordon in 1885. Blunt, with extraordinary foresight, had predicted this event in a letter to Gordon written from Delhi a year before the General's death :

> If the object of your mission is to divide the tribes with a view to retaining any part of the country for the Khedive . . . it is bad work and you will fail . . . Consider what your death will mean : the certainty of a cry for vengeance in England, and an excuse with those who ask no better than a war of conquest.

And in another "secret history", *Gordon at Khartoum* (1912), Blunt showed "that European action alone was the initial cause of the trouble, and that the fanatical character of the Soudanese revolt was due solely to the intervention of the Christian powers at Cairo." And he supported the Arabs with characteristically unpatriotic fervour :

> These English soldiers are mere murderers, and I confess I would rather see them all at perdition than that a single Arab should die . . . [The Arabs are] men with a memory of a thousand years of freedom, with chivalry inherited from the Saracens, the noblest of ancestors, with a creed the purest the world ever knew, worshipping God and serving Him in arms like the heroes of the ancient world they are.

Just as Gladstone had moved from an active sympathy with Balkan and Italian nationalism to a belief in Irish Home Rule, and Casement would later shift from a compassion for the rubber workers in the Congo and the Amazon to a belief in Irish independence, so Blunt, whose plea for Egyptian nationalism was supported by the Irish Members of Parliament, believed that "The two causes, the Irish and the Egyptian, the Catholic and the Mohammedan, stand on a common footing of enlightened humanity, and of that adherence to religious tradition which I held to be essential in every well-ordered community." Blunt was attracted to religious tradition because he saw it as a powerful source of national unity, and he characteristically attributes nationalism more to a desire for spiritual independence than to the common hatred of foreign oppressors.

Blunt's participation in the land war in Ireland came at one of the most crucial moments in Anglo-Irish history, between the defeat of the first Home Rule bill in 1886 and the fall of Parnell in 1890. Gladstone's bill was defeated by thirty votes in what Blunt called "an almost irretrievable disaster" and Lord Salisbury, the new Prime Minister, believed that Ireland needed twenty years of firm and resolute government, so there was a crushing of Irish hopes and a hardening of English policy just before Blunt entered the conflict.

Blunt paradoxically called himself "the last of the Tory Home-Rulers and anti-Imperialists". When he ran for parliament in Camberwell, south of London, in 1885, his outspoken declaration for the restoration of a parliament in Dublin led to his narrow defeat by 162 votes. In the general election of 1886 he again stood as a Liberal candidate for Kidderminster, near Birmingham, and lost again when all the Gladstonian candidates were routed.

Having failed to secure a place in parliament from which to expound his views, Blunt set out to make them known in less orthodox ways. In 1886 he made his first political tour in the disturbed districts of Ireland in order to familiarize himself with the land war (as he had done with imperial conditions in India and Egypt) and "to bring the injustices of the land laws as administered by English insistence on legal ideas, foreign to the traditions and morality of the Irish peasantry, home to the London public." Blunt was an anomalous figure in society, and his hard-headed aristocratic friends thought he was peculiar and perhaps ridiculous. When Blunt told John Morley, the Irish secretary, that he was going to Ireland and did not wish to be arrested, the accommodating Morley "promised he would not. 'Or at any rate,' he said, 'you shall have a luxurious dungeon.' " And his cousin, George Currie, expressed the characteristic upper-class view that the Irish "case is not a serious one, and it is absurd to suppose that the rights of property will be sacrificed to their vagaries."

Blunt's actual experience with conditions in Ireland, as in India and Egypt, intensified his sympathy for oppressed peoples. For Blunt's response to injustice was highly emotional, and he recorded that the sight of dispossessed families "made me so angry that I was positively ill . . . No one can understand the Irish land question till he has seen an eviction . . . I had gone to Ireland a Home Ruler, my tour in the West had made me a Land Leaguer, and the sight of the evictions in Roscommon had made me very near a Fenian."

The land question, which is treated in Joyce Cary's *Castle Corner* (1938), was supremely important in nineteenth century Irish history because it was, in Marx's words, "the exclusive form of the social question in Ireland." The agricultural depression of the 1870s had continued into the 1880s creating a recurring pattern of eviction, agitation and violence that included cattle-maiming, burning and shooting; and in 1880, at the height of the agitation, more than 2,000 families were evicted and 2,600 acts of violence were committed. In 1881 Parnell was imprisoned without trial in Kilmainham jail in Dublin, under the Coercion Laws enacted the previous year. His negotiations with Gladstone in 1882 led to the Kilmainham Treaty in which the Prime Minister promised to settle the problem of arrears in rent and to suspend coercion, and the nationalist agreed to collaborate with the government for Irish reform and to accept the Land Act of 1881.

According to this Act the rents of one third of the Irish tenants were fixed by the land courts. But because of the catastrophic fall of agricultural prices in 1885 and 1886, it became difficult, if not impossible, for the tenants to pay their full rents. In order to protect tenants from unfair evictions, in October 1886 the nationalist leaders William O'Brien and John Dillon launched the Plan of Campaign, a refinement of Parnell's Land League, to compel landowners to reduce the rents by refusing to pay any rent at all until a reduction had been conceded. The English response to the Plan of Campaign was the tougher Coercion Act of 1887 and the appointment of Lord Salisbury's nephew, Arthur Balfour, as Irish Secretary. At first the Irish leaders looked on Balfour as "a silk-skinned sybarite whose rest a crumpled rose-leaf would disturb"; but Ireland quickly transformed him into "Bloody" Balfour, who ruthlessly enforced the Coercion laws and imprisoned Blunt and William O'Brien as well as twenty-two other Irish Members of Parliament under this Act.

At the trial of O'Brien on the charge of inflammatory speechmaking, which took place in September 1887 at Mitchelstown in County Cork, a riot occurred and the police, threatened by the mob, fired on them, killed three men and wounded three others. O'Brien was prosecuted by Edward Carson, who became the political adversary of Roger Casement, and his conviction led to the Battle of Trafalgar Square on November 13th, when Cunninghame Graham was arrested. In April 1887 *The Times* published the Piggott forgeries that attempted to implicate Parnell in the Phoenix Park murders (which had taken place in May 1882 at the peak of the Egyptian crisis), and these lies were not exposed until 1889. Thus, as one historian states, "After 1887 the whole tenor of government policy in Ireland changed, and for the first time Parnellites faced an adversary willing to fight fire with fire."

Curtis' description in *Coercion and Conciliation in Ireland* of Blunt's return to Ireland reveals the typical attitude towards Blunt's political activism :

> One of the most inveterate enemies of coercion in any country was Wilfred Scawen Blunt, who in 1885 claimed the distinction of being a Tory Home Ruler. Few Englishmen were better equipped for martyrdom than this impassioned traveller and man of letters who loved to dress as an Arab sheikh. Having just been a guest along with Balfour at the Wyndhams' family seat, *Clouds* in Wiltshire, this champion of the "backward nations of the world" went to Ireland in October 1887, with the express purpose of defying the Crimes Act.

The force of "inveterate enemies of coercion" is considerably diminished by the somewhat sneering tone of "claimed the distinction," "equipped for martyrdom" and "impassioned traveller"; and the fact that Blunt (like Lawrence) spent many years in the East and felt more comfortable in Arab clothing, has nothing to do with his activities in Ireland. It was entirely characteristic of Blunt, who courted unpopularity, to spend one day with George Wyndham, Balfour's Private Secretary, and the next day leading the Irish peasants in opposition to him. For Blunt states in *The Land War in Ireland* (1912), "I was troubled about Ireland during the night, and have now decided to go. There are so many who have shirked committing themselves that, now it is a case of a real fight with the Government, it would be mean to hold back." In the light of this conscientious choice and Blunt's subsequent actions, it is difficult to doubt the sincerity of his commitment to the Irish cause.

Blunt states that his aim was to test the validity of the Coercion Act, "especially in the matter of forbidding public meetings, which it was thought could be done by placing the Government in the dilemma of having to arrest an Englishman for doing in Ireland what in England was admitted to be the right of every peaceable citizen." Blunt's personal defiance of the government, and his belief that he had a right to hold a meeting in the heart of the most disturbed part of Ireland to protest against a great landlord and express his sympathy with the tenants, became a symbolic test of Balfour's Coercion Act and Salisbury's policy of "resolute government."

As early as January 1886 there had been clear indications on the Galway estates of Hubert, Marquess of Clanricarde, that the evicted tenants would soon become violent. The eccentric Marquess (whom Blunt had known well in the diplomatic service) was a millionaire, a miser and a recluse who lived continuously at the Albany in Piccadilly, had never visited his property of 56,000 acres and had gained notoriety by stating, "If you think you can intimidate me by shooting my agent, you are mistaken."

Though a proclamation by Balfour forbidding the meeting of Clanricarde's tenants was posted in Woodford on October 23, and the village was occupied by 150 constables and a company of Scots Guards, 200 people appeared to hear Blunt speak. Blunt's description in *The Land War in Ireland* of his arrest, just after he had mounted the platform, reveals his tenacious idealism and resolution in the face of attacks by the police. Though Blunt was a poor public speaker, he was only allowed to utter

three words, "Men of Galway!", when a rush was made at me from behind and I found myself suddenly pushed forward off the platform by [Inspector] Byrne and his satellites, who had mounted it at his signal in our rear; my wife and Mrs. Rowlands were swept off by the same impulse . . . Seeing the place otherwise unguarded, I again mounted, followed by Anne, and once more began to speak, though in truth my audience was much too preoccupied with its rough-and-tumble with the police to pay much further attention to me. I was determined, however, that we would not be driven a second time from our position except by actual force, and when Byrne attempted to repeat his manoeuvre gave him as good as I got in the pushing-match that ensued between us, until he had to call for help, when seven or eight of his men ran back and, laying hold of me, dragged me as before to the edge of the platform, from which we all again toppled over together . . . Byrne alone among them was brutal, and towards Lady Anne. Anne during the whole affair obstinately clung to me, and he, seizing her from behind by the throat, hurt her considerably in his attempts to drag her off. Once on the grass and in their hands, I lay there passive, while Anne, who thought me injured, abjured them to stand off; and they would have let me go if I had been so minded. But my mind was now made up to push things to their ultimate issue and force them to arrest me, and while they were hesitating what to do I jumped to my feet and facing a band of them drawn up in front of us, I shouted suddenly: "Are all of you such damned cowards that not one of you dares to arrest me?" This had the desired effect.

The news of Blunt's arrest, in which he challenged all the social conventions of this class war, caused a mild sensation in England. Salisbury wrote to Balfour, "I was delighted to see you had Wilfred Blunt run in"; and his nephew somewhat apologetically explained the circumstances to Lady Elcho: "We are trying to put your cousin in gaol. I have not heard whether we have succeeded. I hope so, for I am sure Blunt would be disappointed at any other consummation, though I should be sorry for Lady Anne who may not hold the same views about political martyrdom as her husband. He is a goodish poet, and a goodish lawn tennis player and a goodish fellow but how bored he must be" to do this. Though Sir Joseph Ridgeway, the Irish Under Secretary, doubted the validity of the case against Blunt, Salisbury recognized that Blunt's exemplary protest demanded an exemplary punishment, that public opinion would support Blunt's prosecution and that "The great heart of the people always chuckles when a gentleman gets into the clutches of the law." Just as Blunt had to goad the police into arresting him, so his rank in society seemed to diminish the force of his gesture. He was not taken seriously by his own class and his act was dismissed as an eccentric desire for martyrdom.

Blunt was tried in Loughrea by two "distinguished magistrates" whom he described as a Limerick grocer and "a decayed racing man, who, on the very day on which he was sentencing me was having judgement delivered against himself for debt in the Court of the Queen's Bench." Blunt was sentenced to two months in prison, appealed and was released on bail. Sponsored by the Liberal party, he made a triumphant political tour of northern England and agreed to stand as a parliamentary candidate for Deptford in south London.

When Blunt returned to Portumna in January 1888 for his appeal trial, which was covered by a special reporter from *The Times,* there was a general illumination in his honour, and a number of people were sent to prison for demonstrating in court. George Lefevre, who attended the trial, relates that numerous evictions continued in the area and that "the whole countryside was in a state of alarm and terror which would be difficult to exaggerate."

Though Balfour described the local courts as "cowardly and corrupt" (that is, pro-Irish), the government made sure that Carson's prosecution would result in Blunt's conviction. For Lefevre reports that the judge, Mr. Henn,

> was completely under the influence of the Crown lawyers; almost without exception, he followed their direction or suggestion in the various legal points which came before him . . . Mr. Henn was evidently determined to do his utmost to prejudice Mr. Blunt in the eyes of the British public and to cover him if possible with ridicule and contempt. Mr. Blunt, in his view, in coming to Woodford was actuated only by a desire of notoriety; he was a vain man of unbalanced judgement . . . It is absolutely certain, therefore, that if Mr. Blunt had been tried by a jury, even a special jury at Dublin, there would have been no conviction.

Blunt was immensely proud of being the first Englishman in history to be imprisoned for taking the Irish side against the English, just as he had been the first Englishman to defend the Indians against the imperialists. When he was brought from Kilmainham jail where he had been transferred in order to testify in his third trial, on the charge he had brought against Inspector Byrne for assaulting him at the Woodford meeting, he also became the first convict to be photographed in prison dress.

The issues in this civil action were the same as in the two previous trials—whether the meeting was lawful and whether the police were justified in dispersing it by force; but though this was a jury trial, Blunt needed a *unanimous* verdict to win. Blunt rightly considered his participation in the land war, and especially his third trial, to be the turning point of his life, for after a conversation with Wyndham in 1906, his Irish memories were still vivid and he recorded:

> We touched upon old times and my campaign in Ireland, and I told him how nearly I had won the campaign against Balfour in 1888 when I was in prison. At my trial in the Four Courts, eleven out of the twelve jurymen were for me; had I secured the twelfth I should have won my case, had I won my case I should have won the Deptford election, and had I won the Deptford election . . . I should have been able to meet Balfour and my other political enemies face to face in the House of Commons and in all probability have satisfied my Old Testament desire of vengeance upon them. Balfour must almost of necessity have resigned the Chief Secretaryship, or at least have abandoned his policy of extreme coercion.

Though there are a great many "ifs" in this statement (as well as in Blunt's entire career) and Blunt tends to exaggerate the possible consequences of his putative victory, it is clear he *was* right in principle and that he *did* get very close to winning both the trial and the election. And there is no doubt that his sympathy, his energy and his intelligence would have made him an extremely effective Member of Parliament.

The Arabist A. W. Kinglake observed "there is a fire about Mr. Blunt which must command a following," and as he passed through the villages on his way to Galway jail he was acclaimed as a patriotic hero with bonfires and torchlight processions. In *The Land War in Ireland* he relates:

> It was a strange emotional sensation to find ourselves thus the object of passionate regard and demonstrative affection among a people embittered against our English nationality by centuries of wrongdoing, and once more the thought surged strongly in me of how noble a thing it was that I should have been called to suffer something,

however little, of ignominy and pain in expiation of my country's crime.

Blunt's desire for expiation was a stronger motive than his supposed quest for martyrdom. Though Blunt was divided between veneration for the traditions of his class and hatred of its injustice, his imprisonment resolved this ambiguity and certified his sacrifice; and he wrote that "Once inside the prison gates a feeling of great peace succeeded in me."

Though Blunt thought his "responsibility for the time was over," he continued his campaign inside the prison. There was no distinction in Ireland between political and common crimes, and Blunt was denied his "luxurious dungeon" and was treated as an ordinary criminal. But he was determined to resist the government's attempt to quell the spirit of English sympathizers who came to Ireland to give their aid and support. Curtis' remark that "the harsh prison rules discouraged many of the rank and file and such sensitive souls as Scawen Blunt from repeating their offences," reveals a total misconception of Blunt's character and motives, for he was quite unlike the rank and file and certainly not a "sensitive soul" when it came to physical hardship. Since his protest against the Coercion laws was a symbolic demonstration of solidarity of sympathy, there would be no point in "repeating the offence." According to Frank Harris, Blunt "would have been let off, because of his position and connections, if he had only promised not to begin again, but he would take no pledge."

While a convict, Blunt also fought for the improvement of prison conditions. Since the regulation dress was inadequate in cold weather he refused to surrender his own coat and had to be forcibly divested of it after special orders had been sent from Dublin. He was also deprived of his large-print Bible, books and writing materials as well as of his handkerchief and toothbrush. He described his treatment in a "Memorandum on Prison Reform" (1910), which he wrote for the Home Secretary, Winston Churchill:

> I was made to wear prison dress, sleep on a plank bed, pick oakum and perform other duties assigned to hard labour prisoners. I was forbidden to receive visits or write letters or have any books to read but a bible and a prayer book except during the last week of my confinement, which was strictly silent and separate during the whole two months . . . The plank bed prevented sleep for more than a very short portion of the long winter nights passed in darkness.

Blunt was generally free from self-pity and tried to make the best of the experience. The friendly warders treated him with a "certain respectful consideration," under the rather lax discipline a fellow prisoner swept out his cell each morning, and he was permitted to sit cross-legged on the floor, which allowed him to imagine himself in the East. He was comforted by a glimpse of sunshine, the jackdaws at his windows and the traditional tame mouse; and he so enjoyed separating the strands of the oakum rope, which he compared to a woman's golden hair, that he hid a bit on Saturday night so that he would not be too bored on the Sabbath. He also managed to compose the sixteen sonnets of *In Vinculis* (1888), which he correctly judged to be "not very good." For the first poem, "Condemned," suffers from an unfortunate comparison with Christ and from what he calls an excess of "black melancholy which nothing could relieve" :

> From Caiphas to Pilate I was sent,
> Who judged with unwashed hands a crime to me,
> Next came the sentence, and the soldiery
> Claimed me their prey. Without, the people rent
> With weeping voices the loud firmament.
> And through the night from town to town passed we
> Mid shouts and drums and stones hurled heavily
> By angry crowds on love and murder bent.
>   And last the gaol.—What stillness in these doors !
> The silent turnkeys their last bolts have shot,
> And their steps die in the long corridors.
> I am done. My tears run fast and hot.
> Dear Lord, for Thy grief's sake I kiss these floors
> Kneeling, then turn to sleep, dreams trouble not.

Blunt also caused a furore among his English friends when contrary to his instinctive feelings and well aware that he would be socially condemned, he committed a serious indiscretion in order to obtain more humane treatment for all political prisoners. When the visiting justices came to inspect his prison, Blunt charged that during the weekend at *Clouds* Balfour boasted of his intention to imprison six weak and unhealthy nationalist leaders in the hope that jail would kill them. When the newspapers published Blunt's story Balfour naturally called it "a ridiculous lie" and the shocked Wyndham thought Blunt was "temporarily out of his senses." But Blunt, who repeated his charge in a letter to *The Times* after his release from prison, must have been telling the truth. For John Manderville, who was jailed with O'Brien in Michelstown, died a few months after his release; and Conor Cruise O'Brien states : "The poor health—usually TB records—of several Irish leaders was at this time, for English politicians, a subject of inexhaustible amusement . . . 'What a lot they are !—Parnell, Dillon, O'Brien, Sexton —all interesting gentlemen in the last stages of debility,' Harcourt wrote to Morley in the summer of 1887."

Though it is impossible to determine the precise effect of Blunt's participation in the land war, some specific improvements were made at the time of his imprisonment. At the end of 1887 an amending bill was passed by the government that allowed the reduction of judicial rents and extended the protection available to tenants, in 1888 another Land Purchase Act increased the amount of money available to tenants for buying their farms, and peasant ownership of land was the solution finally embodied in the Act of 1903, which was passed during George Wyndham's tenure as Irish secretary.

Personally, however, Blunt was profoundly discouraged by his involvement in the land war and the Home Rule movement, and his release from prison in March 1888 marked the close of his active connection with Irish affairs and of his public life in England. For he wrote at that time : "I am in the lowest possible spirits, having come to the extremest end of my political tether, quarrelled with most of my old friends, and got little comfort from the new . . . My interest in politics has slipped away and my power to deal with them . . . As a matter of personal ambition, *politics have nothing more to give me.* I will not be a parliamentary drudge, and I cannot aspire to lead a party." Blunt always saw politics in personal terms so that his parliamentary failure and prison sentence led to his rejection of political life. Deeply grieved by his estrangement from his closest friends and relatives, and deprived of both his old place in society and a new political role, he compared himself to his friend William Morris (whose social commitment was more profound than his own) : "In some ways our two positions were the same. We had both of us sacrificed much socially to our principles, and our principles had failed to justify themselves by results, and we were both driven back on earlier loves, art, poetry, romance."

During the remaining thirty-four years of Blunt's life the opposition of politics and romance intensified as he withdrew from an increasingly hostile and unsympathetic world. For when Blunt was asked to give his idea of heaven, it was

> to be laid out to sleep in a garden, with running water near, and so to sleep for a hundred thousand years, and then to be woke by a bird singing, and to call out to the person one loved best, "Are you there?" and for her to answer, "Yes, are you?" and so turn round and go to sleep again for another hundred thousand years.

In 1886 Blunt found himself disgusted with the emptiness of the world and seriously thought of retiring as a dervish or monk; and eleven years later he made a dangerous pilgrimage to the Senussi monastery of Siwah in the Tripolitan desert in order to realize his dream of a true hermitage. This expedition, which led to physical violence and extreme disillusionment, was, in a strange way, a repetition of Blunt's experiences in Ireland.

After travelling in the desert for more than three weeks Blunt reached his destination only to be attacked by the Siwans whose "better tradition of Islam" he had hoped to discover. Blunt narrates how he was surrounded by a number of men just outside the village and

> though I made no defence except in words, one of them struck me a blow on the side of the neck and others began to try and pull my clothes off me, others pointed guns and pistols at me, and there was a vast hubbub and confusion, one dragging me one way and another another. I received several blows on the head and one from some weapon on the cheek . . . But, strangely enough, I was not at all frightened, and felt interested in it all almost as a spectator . . . The whole thing, with its almost mediaeval and quite barbaric costuming and staging, was more like a pageant than a reality, so that it seemed difficult to realize that it was quite in earnest.

Blunt was beaten, robbed and then released when the Bedouins found out he was an Englishman, and he confesses :

> My experience of the Senussia at Siwah has convinced me that there is *no* hope anywhere to be found in Islam. I had made myself a romance about these reformers, but I see that it has no substantial

basis, and I shall never go farther now than I am in the Mohammedan direction. The less religion in the world perhaps, after all, the
better.

Undaunted by this disappointment Blunt, with Sydney Cockerell (who
later became director of the Fitzwilliam Museum), made another pilgrimage to Mount Sinai in 1900. But their Khedival steamer, carrying
Moslem pilgrims from Suez to Mecca rather like the Patna in *Lord Jim,*
struck a coral reef on the first night. By the next morning waves were
sweeping the upper deck, the wind had increased in violence and it
seemed that the ship would break up. Blunt spent four days on the
reef, sustained by oranges and morphia, until they were finally rescued
by a British gunboat.

At the very height of European imperialism, when gunboats were
used more for diplomacy than rescue, when the French were in North
Africa, the Italians in Libya, the English in Egypt, the Russians in
Persia and the Turks in the Balkans, Blunt assumed the role of a modern
Jeremiah and enjoyed the bitter satisfaction of having his dark predic-
tions come true. In his celebrated diaries, letters to *The Times,* pamphlets
and secret histories, he maintained his reputation for contentious crusades,
expressed his impotent rage at human folly and continued his "individual
protest against the abominations of the Victorian age." As his friend
Cunninghame Graham wrote, mixing classical and biblical references,
"His was a voice as of a Cassandra prophesying in the wilderness, in the
days when he warned England that Egypt would be free, that Ireland
would become a nation, and that our Indian Empire was seething with
revolt. Had he been listened to, the measures that have been wrung
from us by force would have been graciously bestowed."

After meeting Stanley in Cairo in 1887, on his way to relieve Emir
Bey in Zanzibar, Blunt fervently hoped "he may leave his bones half
way. All that Europe has done by its interference of the last thirty
years in Africa had been to introduce firearms, drink and syphilis."
Blunt defended the interests of the Africans (not the Boers or the English)
in the Boer War; and answered the jingoistic poetry of Swinburne and
Kipling with his own rather bombastic and boring *Satan Absolved*
(1899), a dialogue in heaven between God and Satan—sired by Herbert
Spencer out of Goethe—in which Satan complains that mankind has
surpassed him in wickedness.

In *The Shame of the 19th Century* (1900), another corrosive response to Victorian complacency, Blunt noted the "changes in England indicative of moral and material decay corresponding very closely with the ruin we have inflicted on others." He approved of the violent anarchists in the 1905 revolution, and when he heard that the Grand Duke Serge had been blown up by a bomb, he wrote enthusiastically that "Assassination is the only way of fighting a despotism like that of Russia. It shows that the revolutionists mean business."

In *Atrocities of British Justice in Egypt* (1907), Blunt publicly condemned the notorious Denshawi affair in which five Egyptians, who had objected to English officers shooting their pigeons, were wounded by gunshot. The Englishmen were disarmed and beaten by an angry mob, and one of them later died of sunstroke. But a terrible vengeance was exacted for this accidental death : four of the Denshawi villagers were hanged, four were sentenced to life imprisonment and eighteen others were sent to jail or given fifty lashes.

Blunt continued to agitate against the English occupation of Egypt, which was to last for seventy years. When in 1907 he heard that Lord Cromer, the *de facto* ruler of Egypt since 1883, had finally resigned, Squire Blunt felt "like a huntsman at the end of his day's sport with Cromer's brush in my pocket, and the mask of that ancient red fox dangling from my saddle." Blunt addressed the Egyptian National Congress in 1910; and paid for and edited the nationalist magazine, *Egypt,* during 1911 and 1912.

Blunt attacked the "Italian Horrors" in Libya in 1911 and, ironically, suggested that the English send their fleet to drive the Italians out of North Africa. And when the Great War broke out he once again refused to be conventionally patriotic and obstinately followed his anti-imperialistic beliefs to their logical conclusions :

> What especially disgusts me in our taking part in the war is that we should be helping Russia and France and Italy and Belgium, the four nations which have chiefly distinguished themselves for their atrocities in Persia, Morocco, Tripoli and the Congo in recent years. The Germans have been comparatively free of these crimes. And now we have made Kitchener, the hero of the Mahdi's head and the concentration camps in South Africa, dictator here.

Blunt's prewar years, during which he finally published *Gordon at Khartoum* and *The Land War in Ireland,* were also disturbed by a serious deterioration of his health and by intensely bitter and complicated family feuds. These had started in the mid-1890s when Judith learned that her father's affair with a married woman had led to the birth of an illegitimate child. This traumatic discovery changed her attitude toward her father from adoration to contempt, and she confessed, "My child's love for you was worship, the disillusion agony."

Blunt and Lady Anne formally separated in July 1906; and ten weeks later Blunt's mistress, Dorothy Carleton, moved into Newbuildings as his adopted niece and private secretary. But this change led to further conflict, for Miss Carleton and his nurse, Miss Lawrence, were both infatuated with Blunt and extremely jealous of each other. And his deranged daughter Judith—who quarrelled with her mother about the estates and the horses, divorced her husand, broke with her son (Blunt's biographer) and violently attacked her father in the startling pages of *The Authentic Arabian Horse* (1945)—inevitably hated his mistress and told Blunt: "you *know* that your position in regard to Dorothy Carleton is a source of public scandal and of intense pain to my Mother." When Lady Anne died in 1917 the Egyptian stud were sold, the English stud were left to her grandchildren, and Blunt was allowed to keep only six mares. And when Blunt died in 1922 (the year Ireland became independent), his estate was left to Dorothy Carleton. In 1910 Blunt recorded the sensational news of Tolstoy's last days, which must have recalled his own family quarrels and his intense desire to escape from them:

> Tolstoy is dead. A few days ago he ran away from his home, tired to death of his wife and children and announcing his intention of ending his days in a monastery or as a hermit, or anywhere out of reach of them. They had made his life a misery to him by their stupidities, and at the age of 82 he at last broke loose.

Blunt's diary for the years between 1911 and 1914 (when his published journals end) read like a threnody for a dying era, and he often makes a profoundly pessimistic evaluation of his own achievement in life. He believed that he had pursued the sad phantoms of equality and brotherhood, and had "shared the fate of those who have missed their opportunity."

> Today a sad year ends, the worst politically I can remember since the eighties, bloodshed, massacre, and destruction everywhere . . . It has been a losing battle in which I have fought long, but with no

result of good. I am old, and weary, and discouraged, and would
if I could slink out of the fight. I am useless in face of an entirely
hostile world. (1911)

Up to the present moment it had been possible for me to feel that
I had played a useful and successful part in the regeneration of Islam.
Now I can no longer feel this. It is too patent to me that Islam will
never be regenerated, and that my work of thirty years has been
absolutely thrown away. (1912)

A black melancholy is on me caused by a sense of my failure every
where in life. My poetry, my Eastern politics, my Arab horse breeding
were strings to my bow and they have one after another snapped.
(1913)

I realize how little I have accomplished, how little I have affected
the thought of my generation in spite, as I am still convinced, of the
soundness of my view of things, and of some skill and courage in
expounding it. (1914)

There is a truly tragic element in the bitter disappointment of Blunt's
beliefs and hopes, and in his impossible desire to reform not only human
institutions but also human nature.

Blunt was remembered not for what he achieved, but for what he
was and what he represented. In the Preface of *John Bull's Other Island*
(1908) Shaw remarked, "There was Mr. Wilfred Scawen Blunt on the
warpath against tyranny and torture, threatening to get questions asked
in parliament"; and Blunt, who suggested the idea of *The Doctor's
Dilemma,* also served as the model for the handsome and romantic
Hector Hushabye in *Heartbreak House*. In January 1914 Yeats, Pound,
Richard Aldington, Frederick Manning and Sturge Moore recalled
the old days of the Crabbet Club, and gathered at Newbuildings to dine
on roasted peacock and offer Blunt their poetical tribute. Cunninghame
Graham, in his memorial essay, observed that Blunt was "Born out of
his generation, as are the most of men who achieve anything but mere
material success, he yet was a true Englishman, a very Englishman of
the Elizabethan breed, with something in him of the Renaissance in his
love of sport and culture, a combination rare today." E. M. Forster
called Blunt "one of the few noble Englishmen"; and Siegfried Sassoon,
who like Blunt was a minor poet, warrior, wealthy squire and mystic,
and who thought the picturesque, cultivated and aristocratic Blunt "was

the most perfect example of a thoroughbred human being I had seen," has left the finest description of the multifarious adventurer, whom he visited at Newbuildings during his final patriarchal years :

> A strangely beautiful, sensitive old man, with mournfully aged—but wonderfully expressive—eyes . . . I saw him as a proud, many-sided spirit, but capable of tenderness and tolerance. I should like to believe that I saw the essential Blunt—the poet and chivalrous rebel against stupid conventions and political injustice and misgovernment.

For those who did not know him, Blunt is a sad figure because he remained unfulfilled and ineffectual in politics. He had the wrong combination of talents and opportunities, he was limited by his own egoism and vanity, he lacked the patience and dedication for fighting a powerful government, and he became a lonely, disillusioned man. Like Byron, Blunt saw political activity as a way to personal glory and wished to lead a noble people to splendid deeds. His importance lies in his originality, his idealism, his courage, his vivid compassion and his extraordinary prophesies : he was the moral conscience of his age and showed the way toward possibilities of future political action.

ROBERT BONTINE CUNNINGHAME GRAHAM

(1852-1936)

You're a Hamlet choosing to be a Quixote.

CONRAD TO GRAHAM

Ford Madox Ford dramatically described Robert Bontine Cunninghame Graham as "the magnificent prose writer, rightful king of Scotland, head of the clan Graham, Socialist member of parliament and gaolbird." He was also a traveller, horseman, rancher, cattle-dealer, frontiersman, fencing-master, journalist, prospector, historian, Scottish Nationalist and close friend of Wilfred Scawen Blunt, W. H. Hudson and Joseph Conrad.

This colourful figure, admired as a man of action and as a writer by many of the leading intellectuals of his time, spread his talents too thin and achieved very little of enduring importance. Throughout his life Graham had a gift for involving himself in doomed projects and he frequently glorified failure in his work. Shortly after America defeated Spain in 1898 Graham, a great admirer of Spanish culture, wrote in his essay "Success" : "Spain alone still rears its head, the unspoiled race, content in philosophic guise to fail in all she does, and thus preserve the individual independence of her sons . . . Yet those who fail, no matter how ingloriously, have their revenge on the successful few, by having kept themselves free from vulgarity, or by having died unknown." The hyperbole, bravado and insincerity of this rationalization of failure are entirely characteristic of Graham's style and thought. For the works of Unamuno and other intellectuals of the "Generation of '98" prove that Spain was certainly *not* "content to fail," independence does *not* logically follow defeat and failure is *not* a defence against vulgarity.

In a similar passage in "Cruz Alta" Graham stated : "Failure alone is interesting . . . Those who fail after a glorious fashion, Raleigh, Cervantes, Chatterton, Camoens, Blake, Claverhouse, Lovelace, Alcibiades, Parnell, and the last unknown deckhand who, diving overboard after a comrade, sinks without saving him : these interest us." Graham also failed "after a glorious fashion"; but unlike the famous men in his random pantheon whose failures were redeemed by their poetical fame (in this respect they are very different from the unknown diver), Graham's literary success was negligible and he is remembered more for his character and personality than for anything he ever did. Graham's political life follows a pattern manifested both in Blunt and in the lives of many contemporary political activists : a quest for adventure, an espousal of the cause of the oppressed, a brief attempt to work within the conventional political system, followed by disgust, disillusionment and retirement.

Though the House of Lords had denied the claim of Graham's father to the Earldom of Monteith which had expired in 1694, Graham continued to maintain his rather unrealistic claim to the crown of Scotland by descent from the medieval King Robert II, the founder of the Stewart dynasty. Graham's maternal grandfather, Admiral the Honourable Charles Elphinstone Fleeming, commanded the British ships in the West Indies and was the friend of the South American liberators, Bolívar and Páez; and he later represented Stirlingshire in the Reform Parliament. Graham's maternal grandmother was Spanish, and gave birth to his mother on the Admiral's flagship off the coast of Venezuela. In 1845 his father, a wealthy major in the Scots Greys, was thrown from a horse who then kicked him and fractured his skull. This injury damaged his brain and manifested itself in spasms of recklessness and fits of violent temper; and in 1878 the family was forced to confine him in a shooting-lodge where he was cared for by a man-servant.

Graham was born in London in 1852, and learned Spanish at the age of eight when he first visited his relatives in Cadiz. He attended Harrow, which he disliked, during 1864–1866, and then studied languages and fencing at a private school in Brussels. When he was seventeen his parents gave him the money to go into partnership with two Scots who had a ranch in Argentina, and he arrived in Buenos Aires in 1870.

This ranch, like all Graham's capitalistic ventures in the Americas, did not work out very well. Soon after he arrived he was impressed into a revolutionary army, but was released when the brief rebellion expired.

He then left the ranch and invested the last of his funds in five hundred cattle, which he sold in Uruguay for a minute profit. By this time Graham had become an extremely accomplished horseman, and he later celebrated the virtues of the gauchos of the plains with whom he had spent the years of his youth:

> The Llanero is a horseman born. Mounted upon his wiry little steed, ambling along at its artificial pace, he covers sixty miles a day with ease. He swims rivers full of crocodiles and electric eels, lassoes, and breaks an untamed colt, with any horseman in the world . . . Liberty more absolute than that enjoyed by the Llaneros, can rarely have existed upon earth.

In 1871 Graham travelled to Chile and then to Paraguay where, during the previous year, the brutal dictator Francisco Solano Lopez (the future subject of Graham's biography) had been killed in a disastrous war against Argentina, Brazil and Uruguay. The following year Graham was granted a concession from the government of Paraguay to grow *yerba maté,* and returned home where he vainly attempted to form a company to grow this tea. The details of Graham's strenuous life in South America from 1870 to 1878 are not very important, though his enthusiastic authorized biographer, A. F. Tschiffely (who made the famous ride on horseback from Buenos Aires to Washington, D.C.), narrates a series of "perilous journeys," "amazing adventures," "Indian terrors" and "narrow escapes".

In 1878, on his third trip home, Graham met Gabrielle de la Balmondière, who had been born in Chile of French-Spanish parents in 1860 and was now languishing in a Paris convent school. After the briefest courtship they eloped to London, married and went straight to Texas where, as Tschiffely says, "according to rumours and reports, fortunes could be made quickly."

Though others got rich, Graham's hopeless attempts to make money always failed. His plans to breed horses and start a shipping firm came to nothing; and he finally invested in cotton, which he transported by wagon-train from San Antonio to Mexico City. Graham and his wife were attacked by Apaches on this forty-day journey, and by the time they arrived in Mexico City the price of cotton had drastically fallen and they were forced to sell at a loss. Always resourceful, "Professor Bontini" started a fencing academy while Gabrielle taught French, painting and music to well-born ladies.

They returned to San Antonio in 1880 where the "rightful king of Scotland" worked as a shop assistant, horse trainer and journalist, and met Buffalo Bill. In a letter of 1879 Graham expressed characteristic sympathy for the underdog and asked: "Why is it that, in England and America, when white troops win, it is a 'victory', and when beaten it is termed a 'horrible massacre'?" And when in parliament eleven years later, he maintained an active interest in American affairs and protested against the slaughter of the Sioux in South Dakota: "The buffalo have gone first, their bones whitening in long lines upon the prairies, the elk have retired into the extreme deserts of Oregon, the beaver is exterminated to make jackets for the sweater's wife, the Indian must go next."

Graham's adventurous thirteen years in the Americas from 1870 to 1883 determined his character and the course of his career. He learned physical courage and was never afraid of anything. He developed an equestrian expertise and a love of horses that led to the dedication of *The Horses of the [Spanish] Conquest* to his favorite "Pampa" and to the inscription of his old Argentine cattle-brand on his tombstone. He cherished the vigorous and independent code of the gauchos, he understood poor and uneducated people, he valued energy and vitality, he disliked conventional behaviour, he acquired a taste for violence and for revolutionary politics, he gained a breadth of interests and vision, and he absorbed the material and the inspiration for all his later writings. Graham, whom his friends always called Don Roberto, believed that his "outlook on most things in life has been, and is, Spanish." And his aristocratic friend Captain Conrad wrote to him: "I've always felt that there are certain things which I can say to you because the range of your feelings is wider and your mind more independent than that of any man I know."

Graham expressed his manly values in his antithetical biographies of the Paraguayan dictator Lopez and the *conquistador* of Chile, *Pedro de Valdivia*. Lopez, a "bloodthirsty, cowardly tyrant," was notorious for his "cruelty, his cowardice, his monstrous egotism, and his contempt for human dignity"; while Valdivia was "brave to a fault, patient and enduring to an incredible degree, of hardships under which the bravest man might have quailed, loyal to King and Country, and a stout man-at-arms."

In 1883 Graham's deranged father died and he was summoned home to Scotland. Graham first concentrated on the management of his property, which his father had left with a debt of more than £100,000, but he soon became interested in politics. He unsuccessfully contested North West Lanarkshire as an advanced Liberal and Home Ruler in the General Election of 1885 (when Blunt was defeated in Camberwell). But he was returned the following year for the same constituency, which included some dreadful slums in Glasgow, and was a prominent Member of Parliament for six years.

The Times of 1886 called Graham "the aristocratic Socialist and cow-boy dandy," for he came fresh from the pampas to parliament and made a striking impression in London. Frank Harris carefully described him as

> above middle height, of slight nervous strong figure, very well dressed, the waist even defined, with a touch of exoticism in loose necktie and soft hat; in colouring the reddish brown of a chestnut; the rufous hair very thick and upstanding; the brown beard trimmed to a point and floating moustache; the oval of the face a little long; the nose Greek; the large blue eyes.

And in the *Pisan Cantos* Pound speaks of "Mr. Graham himself unmistakably,/on a horse, an ear and the beard's point showing."

Graham was an ideal subject for artists and Jacob Epstein sculpted his bust (now in Manchester), Sir William Rothenstein portrayed him as *The Fencer* (now in New Zealand) and Sir John Lavery painted two equestrian portraits (now in Glasgow and in Buenos Aires). Graham was likened to Van Dyck's portrait of Charles I; and Bernard Shaw, who was fascinated by this vain and "incredible personage", compared him to

> a Spanish hidalgo : hence the superbity of his portrait by Lavery (Velazquez being no longer available). He is, I know, a Scotch laird. How he contrives to be authentically the two things at the same time is no more intelligible to me than the fact that everything that has ever happened to him seems to have happened in Paraguay or Texas instead of Spain or Scotland. He is, I regret to add, an impenitent and unashamed dandy : such boots, such a hat, would have dazzled D'Orsay himself.

Graham, who established the myth of a Spanish hidalgo before he had actually done anything, was better at protests than programmes; and he concentrated as much on maintaining his exotic persona as on achieving his political goals.

Despite his class, wealth, pride and foppishness Graham was, like Blunt, a democratic aristocrat, a Radical with Tory sympathies, an idealist and humanitarian who worked for the welfare of illegitimate children, defended Zulu murderers and fought for the poor, the outcast and the dispossessed. Though John Morley dismissed him as "a professional philanthropist," Ramsay Macdonald believed more accurately that "Graham's Socialism was based on romantic ideas of freedom and his profound feeling for the bottom dog . . . His temperament was that of a soldier of fortune."

Conrad, who knew him best of all, shared his values, used him as a model for the idealistic Don Carlos Gould in *Nostromo* and initiated the extremely adulatory writing about him, always insisted that Graham was a *grand seigneur* born out of his time : "You with your ideals of sincerity, courage and truth are strangely out of place in this epoch of material preoccupations . . . Your aspirations are irrealisable. You want from men faith, honour, fidelity to the truth in themselves and others." But there was also a negative and bitter side to Graham's character (as there was to Blunt's), and as William Rothenstein perceptively observed : "Conrad knew that Cunninghame Graham was more cynic than idealist, that he was by nature an aristocrat, whose socialism was a symbol of his contempt for a feeble aristocracy, and a blatant plutocracy." Even staunch admirers like Edward Garnett and Herbert West speak of Graham's "ice of disdain" and "sardonic contempt for the human race." And David Garnett, who heard Graham address the Subject Races Congress in 1908, writes : "Looking like Charles I, with his aristocratic features and Vandyke beard, and exquisitely dressed, he held up a thin, carefully manicured hand and began his speech with the words : 'I am not one of those who tremble at the word—ASSASSINATION !' " Garnett remarks that "When he made a speech or wrote a book he adopted a pose, and his vanity overcame him"; and this artificiality and egoism combined with disdain and contempt help to explain Graham's failure in both politics and art.

Graham's political ideas were extraordinarily far-sighted. He crusaded against English imperialism, capital and corporal punishment, royalties on mineral rights, commercial profiteering, the sweating system, child labour, religious instruction in schools, the Established Church and the House of Lords. And he supported Home Rule in Ireland and Scotland, universal suffrage, prison reform, nationalization of land and mines, graduated income tax, the eight-hour working day, free secular education, Sunday opening of museums and triennial parliaments. Though he was a colleague of Bernard Shaw, William Morris, H. M. Hyndman, Keir Hardie and John Burns in the great era of English Socialism, he was the only Socialist Member of Parliament. He could introduce these progressive measures into the public and parliamentary mentality, but he was too far ahead of his time to implement them. Graham fought hard for his principles but was basically pessimistic. In later years he remarked that "Like the Liberal Party, which was ground out between the Tories and the Socialists, so is the Socialist Party doomed to be ground out between the Tories and the Communists." This statement led to Tschiffely's shrewd observation : "The Socialist Party originally attracted him because he subconsciously had a feeling it would finally end in failure."

The hard hidalgo lived in the passionate character of his words, and in his maiden speech in parliament in 1886 he opposed a bill to construct a railway in the Lake country (which was passed) and condemned government policy in England, Egypt and Ireland. He complained that in the Queen's speech there was "not one word to bridge over the awful chasm existing between the poor and the rich; not one word of kingly sympathy for the sufferers of the present commercial and agricultural depression—nothing but platitudes, nothing but views of society through a little bit of pink glass." He asked when the troops in Egypt would "be withdrawn from their inactivity in that pestilential region and from playing the ungrateful role of oppressors of an already downtrodden nationality." And he remarked with heavy irony that "far from turning [the Irish tenants] out on a bleak, cold winter's night, the landlord had provided his dependants with a fire to warm their hands; only, through a pardonable inadvertence, it was their houses that had furnished the blaze."

Graham, who was notorious for his unconventional behaviour, gave his most famous parliamentary performance on December 1, 1888 during a debate on the desperate conditions of the chainmakers of Cradley Heath, near Birmingham. Graham had asked the First Lord of the Treasury if he would name a day to discuss a Motion concerning the chainmakers and then declared :

> Graham : If he does not do so, I characterize the Motion as a dishonourable trick to avoid discussion.
> Mr. Speaker : Order ! Order ! The Honourable Member is conducting himself in a most unusual and unparliamentary manner in making use of language of that kind. I must request him to withdraw the expression he has made use of.
> Graham : *I never withdraw.* I simply said what I mean . . .
> Mr. Speaker : Then I must ask the Honourable Member to withdraw from the House.
> Graham : Certainly Sir; I will go to Cradley Heath.

Shaw was so impressed by Graham's indignant retort to parliamentary hypocrisy that he gave the phrase to his hero Major Sergius Saranoff. After expressing surprise that Graham had ever got into the House of Commons, Shaw remarked in his Notes to *Captain Brassbound's Conversion* :

> How he did it I know not; but the thing certainly happened, somehow. That he made pregnant utterances as a legislator may be taken as proved by the keen philosophy of the travels and tales he has since tossed to us; but the House, strong in stupidity, did not understand him until in an inspired moment he voiced a universal impulse by bluntly damning its hypocrisy . . . The shocked House demanded that he should withdraw his cruel word. "I never withdraw," said he; and I promptly stole the potent phrase for the sake of its perfect style, and used it as a cockade for the Bulgarian hero of Arms and the Man.

Graham wanted "to see an extension of the most precious boon men can give one another—namely, sympathy." He went to Cradley Heath, which Disraeli had called a "Hell Hole," and helped to ameliorate the conditions of the chainmakers who worked up to fifteen hours a day for six shillings a week. This was his only real achievement in parliament. His plea for the chainmakers is one of the best things he wrote, for when he abandoned his vanity and affectation he could convey a sympathetic indignation that equals in intensity Orwell's *The Road to Wigan Pier* :

I have never gone to Cradley Heath without coming away in the lowest spirits. The mud is the blackest and most clinging, the roads the slushiest and ruttiest, the look of desolation the most appalling, of any place I have ever seen . . . [Cradley Heath represents] failure of civilisation to humanise; failure of commercialism to procure a subsistence; failure of religion to console; failure of Parliament to intervene; failure of individual effort to help; failure of our whole social system.

Despite the neat parallels, Graham's judgment of society in terms of human dignity is impressive.

Graham's most significant political action was in the Battle of Trafalgar Square on Bloody Sunday, November 13, 1887. The London Radicals and Socialists had been using Trafalgar Square for open-air meetings since 1884 and there had been several clashes with the police. After the riots of February 1886 Blunt wrote rather perversely: "I confess it delights me and I am only sorry I did not wait in Trafalgar Square to see the doings." And in a parliamentary speech of May 1887 Graham attacked the disruption of Socialist meetings by the police: "I believe that these Socialists have been dispersed in their meetings simply and solely because they are poor, because their doctrines are not popular, and because no one cares to stand up and incur the odium of speaking for them." But Graham did not recognize the systematic nature of the oppression of the poor and believed that evils could be remedied if only a chivalric individual would take the risk of speaking out. He failed to see that Socialism was not merely an unpopular doctrine, but also a rationale for organizing working-men to defend their rights and threaten the power of their rulers. Graham's behaviour on Bloody Sunday, when this class warfare erupted and the police inevitably protected the interests of the upper class, revealed both his rash and impulsive nature, and his ineffectuality as a political leader.

In September 1887, as we have seen, William O'Brien, M.P. and other Irish patriots were imprisoned under the Coercion Laws for agitating for Home Rule, and in October Blunt was convicted for speaking at a prohibited meeting of the Clanricarde estate. In order to emphasize the distinction between common criminals and men jailed for political offences O'Brien refused to clean his cell in Tullamore jail or to wear prison clothing, even after his own clothes had been taken from him; and his protest eventually won special privileges for political prisoners.

In London the Metropolitan Radical Federation planned a meeting on November 13th to demand the release of O'Brien and the other Irish leaders. But the Commissioner of Police, Sir Charles Warren, was anxious to terminate these gatherings in Trafalgar Square and prohibited the meeting. Like Blunt, Graham was determined to test the legality of the prohibition, and he marched to the Square with Shaw, Morris, Prince Kropotkin, Edward Carpenter, John Burns, Annie Besant and 50,000 workers, many of whom were jobless and hungry. Curtis writes that "Although the meeting in Trafalgar Square was held ostensibly to protest the imprisonment of William O'Brien, the size and vehemence of the crowd showed that the workingmen of London were more troubled by 'hard times' than by Coercion in Ireland."

The accounts of exactly what happened on Bloody Sunday vary considerably according to the politics and sympathies of the narrators. But they all agree that 1,500 constables were posted around the Square to keep it clear, and that 2,500 police as well as 600 Grenadier and Life Guards were kept in reserve. According to the conservative *Illustrated London News*, "The Mob, who were armed with iron bars, pokers, gas-pipes, short sticks, and even knives, *attacked the police* with fury"; and Graham, who led a column of 400 men into battle, "used his fists freely," "received a blow on the head, inflicting a wound which bled" profusely, was arrested and charged at Bow Street Station.

The Times rejoiced that the "ruffianly mob" had been utterly routed; and its official report, which does not mention Graham's wound, recalls the recent campaigns in the Sudan:

Soon after 4 o'clock things were at their height in the vicinity of Trafalgar Square, and a desperate and concerted attempt was made to break through the police into the centre. About 200 men, headed, it is said, by Mr. Cunninghame Graham, M.P., rushed across from the corner of the Strand near Morley's Hotel and went full tilt at the police, who were drawn up four deep at the corner of the Square opposite. It was a very determined onslaught and evidently made by men acting together according to a *preconcerted plan*. For a few moments there was a hand-to-hand tussle and fists were to be seen uplifted high and being freely used. Some of the attacking party had sticks, but it was mainly a battle of fists. The police momentarily lost ground owing to the rush of their opponents, and it seemed as if the line would be broken and an entrance effected. Other constables, however, were soon at the rescue and the attackers were beaten back. A moment later they were in full retreat.

After what *The Times* editorial called Graham's "insane rush," fifty prisoners were arrested and 150 wounded were taken to hospitals. At 4.30 two reserve squadrons of Life Guards rode up from Whitehall with a magistrate carrying the Riot Act, charged with drawn sabres and finally dispersed the crowd.

But other sources more sympathetic to Graham and his cause emphasize the defeated rather than the dangerous aspect of the crowd. Shaw speaks of a crusading Graham "personally and bodily assailing civilization as represented by the concentrated military and constabular forces of the capital of the world". And Tschiffely relates that when Graham broke through the police lines with John Burns, "a crowd of policemen attacked the two, batoning and kicking them unmercifully. Don Roberto's head was cracked open."

Charles Finger's eye-witness account describes a confused rather than a preconcerted charge that quickly fizzled out when confronted by the armed and disciplined policemen:

Cunninghame Graham, fired by a sudden flame of resentful anger, turned and said something . . . and those nearest him set up a shout. So there came a surging forward, with Graham and Burns in the forefront, and then a confused running. Once I saw Graham, saw his hatless head and bushy hair as he assailed the police. Someone struck him with a sword. But the Londoners had neither the heart nor the courage to follow him, so the end of the attack came with the same rough mauling of the two leaders who were seized by a dozen hands and then taken captive into the middle of the hollow square.

After a conversation with Morris, who based chapter 17 of *News From Nowhere* (1890) on the Battle of Trafalgar Square, Blunt also commented on his friend's disillusionment with the frightened crowd: "He never got over the pusillanimity they had shown at the Trafalgar Square meeting two years before, when a few hundred policemen had dealt with thousands of them as though they had been schoolboys. Morris was too loyal and too obstinate to abjure his creed, but the heart of his devotion to the cause of the proletariat had gone."

Another eye-witness, the artist Walter Crane, reports the battle as an outright slaughter :

I never saw anything more like real warfare in my life—only the attack was all on one side . . . The Guards were called out, and I remember in the high gloom of that November evening the glitter of the bayonets, and the red line in front of the National Gallery, and also the magistrate riding up Parliament Street in the midst of a company of Life Guards, having hastily been fetched to read the Riot Act.

Graham's moving narrative in the Socialist newspaper *The Commonweal* claimed that the police actually dragged him *into* the square by the hair, but this must have been after his charge. He emphasized that the brutality of the police was inspired by their fear and that the gladiatorial spectacle provided Sunday entertainment for the ecstatic upper-classes :

I saw repeated charges made at a perfectly unarmed and helpless crowd : I saw policemen not of their own accord, but under orders of their superiors, repeatedly strike women and children; I saw them invariably choose those for assault who seemed least able to retaliate. One incident struck me with considerable force and disgust. As I was being led out of the crowd a poor woman asked a police inspector (I think) or a sergeant if he had seen a child she had lost. His answer was to tell her that she was a "damned whore" and to knock her down . . . Other things I saw pleased me better than this. I saw that the police were afraid; I saw on more than one occasion that the officials had to strike their free British men to make them obey orders . . . The tops of the houses and hotels were crowded with well-dressed women, who clapped their hands and cheered with delight when some miserable and half-starved working man was knocked down and trodden under foot.

Gabrielle Graham wrote to *The Times,* with some exaggeration, that "Neither my husband nor Mr. Burns resisted in any way, and stood perfectly quiet to be murdered". But she justly complained that "Mr. Cunninghame Grahame was not released on bail last night. He had to wait five hours, ill, feverish, and wounded before the charge was preferred against him. We had bail all ready, but it was refused, and he passed the night in the cells as if he had been a common street thief." And Crane notes that "Graham's health had suffered while in durance, and that public speaking was trying for him, and he nearly broke down on one occasion."

R. B. Haldane, the future Lord Chancellor, eventually stood bail for Graham, and on the day of his trial his wife sent out witty invitations which read:

> Mrs. Cunninghame Graham
> At Home
> Old Bailey.

Graham was defended by his friend and fellow M.P. Herbert Asquith, the future Liberal Prime Minister, but was sentenced to six weeks ordinary imprisonment. According to Lavery, Graham considered hard labour "less irksome than ordinary imprisonment, for with the former you were given plenty of coarse food, and the time passed; while with the latter you were starved and left to pass the time in contemplation." Blunt, who thought it was "much worse in an English prison," sent fraternal greetings from Galway Jail.

After his release from prison in February 1888 Graham was asked what he had learned there and replied: "A deeper sense of the misery of the lives of many of our poor people." Graham's experience in prison inspired one of his best works, "Sursum Corda" (Lift Up Your Heart), which revealed that prison had merely increased his generous sympathy for the wretched of the earth and for what he called the "captives shut within themselves and tortured by the thought that those outside have lost them from their minds".

> How crass it is to shut men up in vast hotels, withdrawing them from any possible influence which might ever change their lives, and to confine them in a white-washed cell, with windows of Dutch glass, gas, a Bible, table, chair, little square salt-box, wooden spoon, tin pan, schedule of rules, hell in their hearts, a pound of oakum in their hands, condemned to silence and to count the days . . .
> The only humanising influence in a prison comes from the prisoners . . . [for] prisoners of whatever rank or class, imprisoned for whatever crime, offence, or misdemeanour, look on each other as old friends after a day or two within the prison walls.

The catalogue of grim detail in this passage is redeemed by Graham's sense of human solidarity and a concept of decency that is similar to Orwell's.

The significance of the Battle of Trafalgar Square has also been variously interpreted by modern historians. Ensor stresses the acrimony engendered by the violence : "The affair is worth recording as the most considerable *émeute* in London during the latter half of the nineteenth century. Bitter memories of it lasted in the working-class districts for over twenty years. Much odium fell on Warren, who was indeed largely to blame." Curtis notes the economic aspects of this virulent class war : "Too few observers interpreted the battle of Trafalgar Square as but another symptom of the endemic disease that was affecting the whole British economy." But Pelling is most perceptive when he emphasizes that Bloody Sunday failed to advance the cause of the Socialist movement :

> After 1887 the danger of violence was reduced as the immediate depression wore off and the numbers of unemployed decreased. The Socialist bodies began to find that they had achieved remarkably little for all the energy they had expended. On the one hand, respectable people were afraid to join their organisation; on the other hand, the unemployed were too poor to subscribe. The Socialists had got a great deal of publicity but very few new members. Moreover, the success of the demonstrations in intimidating the government and the upper classes was very limited; if there was a lesson to be drawn from the events of 1886 and 1887, it was that unarmed workers could not stand up to soldiers and police.

Graham's bold charge into four lines of constables brought him a cracked skull, a jail sentence, more notoriety than sympathy and some posthumous fame. He was determined to oppose the prohibition of the meeting, and when confronted with the phalanx of police he had (like a bull) the options of retreating, which was unthinkable ("I never withdraw") or charging, which was hopeless. He did make a courageous and symbolic gesture of protest, which was all he could do in the circumstances, but he failed to hold the meeting, to obtain the release of O'Brien or to further his own political career.

After his prison term he defended himself in a speech to parliament and declared : "I have been tried on three counts : assault on the police, causing riot, and illegal assembly. However, the good sense and honesty of the British jury acquitted me instantly on the counts of 'assault' and 'riot' . . . I was found guilty of the obsolete offence of illegal assembly."

Despite this attempt to justify his actions Graham felt that the Members of Parliament did not give him a "fair show"; and his defiance of lawful authority, which *The Times* had called "a diseased craving for notoriety, which the charitable may describe as fanaticism," intensified his isolation from his respectable colleagues and accentuated his superficial bravado and his profound contempt.

In 1888 the doughty Graham was beaten and thrown into a canal for supporting a strike of the Clydeside shipworkers; and by 1891 he had become intensely angry and frustrated by what he called "the string-pulled member-marionettes" in the House of Commons. As Pelling writes :

> Graham was well aware of the difficulties of his own position as the only Socialist in Parliament. This Scottish aristocrat, for all the mordant wit of his speeches which revealed the promise of a literary future, was really quite unsuited to political life . . . He represented nobody—not even, now, his own constituency—and it was natural for him to be dismissed as a mere "cowboy dandy" as *The Times* put it. He admitted his weakness to Burns, and urged him to consult with Hardie on that subject. "The House," he said, "is beginning to find out that there is nothing and nobody behind me. Anyone but the idiots in Parliament would have seen this long ago."

Graham founded the Scottish Labour Party with Keir Hardie in 1890. But after he was defeated for re-election as a Labour candidate in 1892 he angrily renounced politics and cynically admitted : "I have been foolish enough to soil myself with the pitch of politics, and to have endured the concentrated idiocy of the Asylum for Incapables at Westminster for six years." And he later remarked that "The dunghill of active politics is a young man's game . . . and it is a dunghill; I know, for I have been on (or in) the hill." Graham was an activist who demanded immediate results and was unable to effect concrete reforms. The democratic process took too long for his impatient spirit.

Though he did not give up Socialist politics entirely, Graham was more renowned as a traveller and writer during the final phase of his life. In 1894 Graham and Gabrielle got carried away after reading Pliny's account of a Roman gold mine in northern Spain and set out at once to find the treasure. But this fantastic scheme, like their earlier ones, was a fiasco. A more celebrated expedition and the subject of Graham's best book, *Mogreb-el-Acksa* (The Far West), was his attempted journey in 1897 to the forbidden city of Tarudant, on the far side of the Atlas Mountains in Morocco, which had excluded Europeans because of its mineral wealth.

Graham's lively, unpretentious but episodic book extolled the values of his early life when men "mounted on a good horse, a rifle in their hands, and a long road to travel for no special cause" were as rich as kings. Graham valued the culture of the Arab as well as of the European race and attempted to "conjure up the best part of all travel— its melancholy." He left Mogodor with three Arab companions, and after travelling south for two hundred miles was arrested by the Caid of Kintafi and detained for twelve days. Though he failed to reach Tarudant, Graham philosophically wrote :

> [We were] well treated, but uncertain of how long we should be kept in honourable captivity, growing more anxious every moment, and yet with something comic in the situation; nothing to do but make the best of it, eat, drink, and sleep, and stroll about, talk with the natives, sit in our tent, and read el Faredi [a medieval poet], giving ourselves up with the best grace we could, to watching and to prayer . . . The strange entrancing half-feudal, half-Arcadian life, which I have seen but for a fortnight, consoled me for my failure.

Mogreb-el-Acksa aroused considerable comment and established Graham's literary reputation when it was published in 1898. Blunt, who had travelled extensively in Arabia, generously wrote : "Your book on Morocco has amused and interested me more than anything of the kind I have read for a long day. I put it next to Doughty's as a true portrait of Arab ways, and far before anything that Burton did." T. E. Lawrence, whom Blunt later introduced to Graham, was more critically perceptive and expressed a patronizing yet convincing point of view :

> Graham's pen swaggers too : and he cannot therefore sustain a book : though he writes the best five or six pages imaginable . . . A wonderful old man. *Maghreb el Aksa* was his most ambitious effort at book writing, and after it he relapsed into his proper role, of filling albums with snapshots—the best verbal snapshots ever taken, I believe. Not much brain, you know, but a great heart and hat : and what a head of hair !

The most enthusiastic response came from Shaw, who bombarded Graham with questions about his journey and used *Mogreb-el-Acksa* as the basis for *Captain Brassbound's Conversion* (1899):

> Somebody told him of Tarudant, a city in Morocco in which no Christian had ever set foot. Concluding at once that it must be an exceptionally desirable place to live in, he took ship and horse; changed the hat for a turban; and made straight for the sacred city, via Mogodor. How he fared, and how he fell into the hands of the Cadi of Kintafi, who rightly held that there was more danger to Islam in one Cunninghame Graham than in a thousand Christians, may be learned from his account of it in Mogreb-el-Acksa, without which Captain Brassbound's Conversion would never have been written.

Graham had published his first book, *Notes on the District of Monteith, For Tourists and Others* in 1895; and during the last forty years of his life he tossed off two hundred short stories and sketches, more than half of them for Frank Harris's *Saturday Review,* and eleven histories of South America. His autobiographical works resemble Bret Harte's, for he was a man of action who wrote about men of action, but the spontaneous and often pointless violence in his fiction comes from nowhere and leads to nothing. Harris justly called Graham "an amateur of genius" who did not take his work seriously; and Ford agreed that Graham, whose book sales were very small, "was aristocratically negligent of the fate of the products of his muse and has remained fittingly little known." Graham creates his finest work when he abandons the disastrously arch and posturing persona of a rakish yet somewhat sentimental literary gaucho, and writes affectingly about the death of his friends: Wilfred Scawen Blunt, Charles Stewart Parnell, William Morris ("With the North-West Wind"), and Joseph Conrad ("Inveni Portum"). He is also excellent in his passionate polemics against racism ("Niggers"), prisons ("Sursum Corda"), industrial exploitation ("The Nail-and-Chainmakers") and police brutality ("Bloody Sunday").

Graham's histories were mainly written after the Great War and largely inspired by his youthful adventures when he "saw the country as I have described, travelled its solitudes, and passed nights alone in its deserted villages." He was fascinated by the religious enterprises of the early Jesuit missionaries which were conducted under great adversity;

and he was strangely complacent and insensitive about the extraordinary cruelty and genocide of the *conquistadores* who, he admitted in a Conradian echo, "plundered and slew, all in God's name, holding, just as we do ourselves, that they were chosen to bring light into the darkest places of the world." Graham's histories are boring, repetitious, sprinkled with pointless and distracting footnotes and weak in form and style ("There, in addition there is the plague of insects, locally called 'La Plaga', that is the plague"). They are neither analytical nor original and often consist of poor translations from the Spanish sources in Buenos Aires or Caracas. As D. H. Lawrence states in his brief but masterful condemnation : "Don Cuninghame, alas, struts feebly in the conquistadorial footsteps . . . He writes without imagination, without imaginative insight or sympathy, without colour, and without real feeling . . . He lifts a swash-buckling fountain pen, and off he goes. The result is a shoddy, scrappy, and not very sincere piece of work."

After the turn of the century Graham suffered two serious losses. In 1903 he was forced to sell Gartmore, which had belonged to his family since 1680; and more grievously, his wife, who had written the life of St. Teresa and translated the poems of St. John of the Cross, died in Hendaye on the Spanish-French border in 1906.

When the war broke out Graham was given the rank of Colonel and sent to Argentina to buy horses for the British Army; and he relates, "I was also in Colombia for nearly a year [in 1917], examining the cattle resources of that republic, with a view of putting up a Packing House for the British Government. Shortage of ships caused the scheme to fall through."

In 1918 Graham was defeated as an Independent Liberal for West Stirlingshire in an election that cost him £900. In 1928 he joined the Scottish National Party, but that movement failed to inspire the enthusiasm of the Scottish people. (His mother, to whom he was deeply attached, died at 93 in 1925.) And he lost the Rectorial elections of Glasgow University in 1928 and again in 1935. He continued to turn out his superficial histories and to travel in South America, Ceylon and South Africa during the winter. On his final trip to Buenos Aires he visited the birthplace of his friend W. H. Hudson, a great authority on Argentina, who in 1920 had generously dedicated *El Ombú* "To Robert Bontine Cunninghame Graham, *singularisimo escritor inglés*, who has lived and knows (even to the marrow as they themselves say), the horsemen of the Pampas, and who alone of European writers has rendered something of the vanishing colour of that remote life." Graham died in Buenos Aires in 1936 at the age of 83, and was buried on an island in the Lake of Monteith.

Blunt and Graham, who knew each other well, had similar characters, experiences, talents and ideas. Both were well-born, wealthy, energetic, impulsive, vain, flamboyant and theatrical aristocrats, and both were models for Shavian heroes. Both had spent years of their early life in Spain and South America, admired Spanish culture, were expert and authoritative horsemen, had travelled extensively in Arab countries, developed a hatred of English imperialism and opposed their own class by advocating nationalist principles. In his last speech in the House of Commons in 1892 Graham called the recently disgraced Parnell "the most remarkable man who sat in [parliament] in this century"; and in 1908 Blunt urged Graham to "take up my work in Egypt for me, as I am really past my day of being of any use there. You have done so much in the past in other directions that I think nobody could do the Egyptian and Indian propaganda better." Both men had an emotional need to protest, were imprisoned at the same time for the same offence, suffered an extreme disillusionment, and devoted themselves to rather amateurish writing, despite their lack of popularity and recognition, for the rest of their long lives.

Blunt was more conservative, serious, sophisticated, intelligent and committed than Graham; and though Graham, unlike Blunt, was elected to parliament, he is most clearly distinguished from his friend by the consistent failures in his life. William Rothenstein relates that during their travels in Morocco in 1894 "Graham, to impress [the Moors], had me throw oranges into the air, at which he shot. Not one of them did he hit." This minor yet characteristic incident is a perfect illustration of Graham's incompetent bravado, for the Moors never bothered to examine the oranges and Graham swaggered off after his impressive performance.

Graham failed as a rancher, horse-dealer, tea planter and cotton trader; as a Socialist agitator and parliamentarian; as a gold prospector and traveller to Tarudant; as a cattle-buyer, historian, Scottish Nationalist and Rectorial candidate; and even as a marksman at oranges. But he is still rightly remembered for his picturesque character, his daring contempt for authority, his sympathy for the oppressed and his fight for humanitarian causes that prepared the way for future progress. For the man Conrad praised as "a most hopeless idealist . . . living half a century, or even more, ahead of his time," believed with Montaigne that the result of an action matters less than the action itself.

ROGER CASEMENT

(1864-1916)

It's a glorious death, to die for Ireland.

ROGER CASEMENT

For a brief moment during the Easter rebellion, the personal fate of Roger Casement was linked with the destiny of a nation, and his complex character and career illuminate that particular phase of Irish history. His efforts on behalf of the rubber workers in the Congo and the Amazon brought him fame and a knighthood, but his attempt to aid Ireland led him to the gallows. His role in the independence movement was a paradigm of noble yet pathetic heroism, and his execution for high treason in August 1916 a moral and political tragedy. The pattern of his political life, a series of disasters that testify to his compulsive desire for death and martyrdom, suggests profound guilt about his homosexuality and a need for self-punishment. His private diaries were more fantastic than real, and he was hanged for his sexual as well as his political dreams.

Roger David Casement was born in Dublin on September 1, 1864. His father, a Protestant captain in the Antrim militia who had fought with Kossuth in the Hungarian revolution, died when he was six. His mother, a Catholic, died three years later, and the orphan boy was then brought up as a Protestant by an uncle in northern Ireland, and educated at Ballymena Academy. He became a clerk in a Liverpool trading company when he was eighteen, and two years later, in 1884, he sailed for Africa where he served King Leopold's Congo Free State as an explorer, hunter, surveyor and administrator. He returned to England after five years of service, but was sent out again the following year to organize transport on the Lower Congo for the Belgian authorities. At this time Casement first met Joseph Conrad, who was running his "tin-pot steamboat" on the Congo River, and in a letter to Cunninghame Graham the novelist later described Casement with amazed respect as a Protestant Irishman, pious too. But so was Pizarro. For the rest I can assure you that he is a limpid personality. There is a touch of the conquistador in him too; for I've seen him start off into an unspeakable wilderness swinging a crookhandled stick for all weapons, with two bulldogs, Paddy (white) and Biddy (brindle), at his heels and a Loanda boy carrying a bundle for all company. A few months afterwards it so happened that I saw him come out again, a little leaner, a little browner, with his stick, dogs and Loanda boy, and quietly serene as though he had been for a stroll in the park.

Casement was a tall, extremely handsome man, of fine bearing, a muscle and bone thinness, wrinkled forehead, face deeply tanned from long tropical service, thick, curly black hair, full and long pointed beard, and brilliant blue eyes.

With his impressive and responsible experience in the Congo, the young Casement entered the service of the Nigerian Protectorate in 1892, and three years later he was appointed Her Majesty's Consul in the Portuguese colony of Mozambique. In Lourenço Marques, Casement first exhibited his eccentric patriotism and was officially reprimanded for using stationery marked "Consulate of Great Britain and Ireland." After serving in Angola on the west coast, he was employed during the Boer War on special service in Capetown, for which he received the Queen's South African medal. In 1900, when he was appointed Consul at Boma in the Congo Free State, Wilfred Blunt wrote: "The King of the Belgians has invested his whole fortune on the Congo, where he is brutalizing the negroes to fill his pockets . . . The whole white race is revelling openly in violence, as though it had never pretended to be Christian. God's equal curse be on them all!" And in 1903 Casement conducted the investigation of atrocities committed upon the rubber workers in the Upper Congo which brought him world-wide fame.

During this investigation Casement kept the first of his extant diaries, which were to play such a notorious and fatal part in the last year of his life. He was extremely responsive to the natural beauty of the country, and as he rode through the jungle on the flooded, swollen river he sighted splendid blue Emperor butterflies, coloured macaws, tiny chattering green parrots, a black and white Egyptian ibis in full flight, and the lively monkeys screaming eternally in the trees. In the evening the children bathed in the river, and stars cooled the sky in the night.

These physical surroundings provided a strong contrast to the terrible atrocities committed upon what Casement called "the poor, the naked, the fugitive, the hunted, the tortured, the dying men and women of the Congo." Africans, bound with thongs that contracted in the rain and cut to the bone, had their swollen hands beaten with rifle butts until they fell off. Chained slaves were forced to drink the white man's defecations, hands and feet were chopped off for their rings, men were lined up behind each other and shot with one cartridge, and wounded prisoners were eaten by maggots till they died and were thrown to starving pie dogs or devoured by cannibal tribes. One girl carried the bones of her parents clinking in a ragged canvas sack and testified that starving people ate peeling whitewash torn from old buildings and then vomited up a green bile filled with leeches. Another boy described to Casement how during a raid on his village he was wounded and "fell down, presumably insensible, but came to his senses while his hand was being hacked off at the wrist. I asked him how it was he could possibly lie silent and give no sign. He answered that he felt the cutting, but was afraid to move, knowing that he would be killed, if he showed any sign of life."

Though he had official sanction from the King's government in Brussels, Casement suffered daily obstructions by the officials of the State whose very existence was threatened by his inquiries. He wrote to his friend Richard Morten that Africa "has been 'opened up' (as if it were an oyster) and the Civilizers are now busy developing it with blood and slaying each other, and burning with hatred against me because I think their work is organized murder, far worse than anything the savages did before them." His detailed record of the atrocities achieved great force through its moderate tone and objective style, which expressed Casement's passionate commitment to the oppressed. As he wrote to Edmund Morel, the founder of the Congo Reform Association: "if I get home again I should go to all lengths to let my countrymen know what a hell upon earth our own white race has made, and was daily making, of the homes of the black people it was our duty to protect."

After Casement had sacrificed his health to complete the report, he found further obstructions from his own government. Some men in the Foreign Office, ignorant about the actual conditions in the Congo, felt that Casement had exaggerated his findings, and when the report was published, their "method of conducting the controversy with Leopold consisted largely in running away from their own charges and offering apologies for my report . . . They shove me into the forefront, bitterly against my will—promising, too, that they would stick up for me—and then they shrink off and leave me exposed to vulgar abuses and openly expressed contempt . . . They are not worth serving, and what sickens me is that I must go back to them, hat in hand, despising them as I do, simply to be able to live."

Casement believed, with considerable justification, that he was becoming the pawn of political interests while the tyranny in the Congo continued unchecked. He was chosen to conduct the inquiry, and then "humiliated, insulted, deserted" after it was published. As an Irishman, he had felt a natural sympathy for the Boers in the South African War; and he became bitterly hostile to the British government when it betrayed and abandoned him. But in 1908, after the creation of the Congo Reform Association, Casement triumphed; and world opinion, finally stirred by his discoveries, forced King Leopold to surrender his personal ownership of the Congo Free State, which became a colony of Belgium. Casement was rewarded by his government and made Commander of St. Michael and St. George.

In 1906 his consular career shifted to South America when he was appointed Consul at Santos and at Para in Brazil, and then Consul-General in Rio de Janeiro; and in 1910 he was asked to conduct another investigation of atrocities committed upon the rubber workers in the Putumayo region of the Peruvian Amazon. Casement's experiences in the Amazon were a nightmarish repetition of the Congo. Here, as in Africa, an immense river, cutting through a remote jungle far from government control, was used to transport rubber collected by natives, who were enslaved and brutalized by their white overseers. Casement reported that the Indian, with his gentle face, soft black eyes and far-off look of the Incas, was so terrified and "so humble that as soon as he sees that the needle of the scale does not mark the [required] 10 kilog., he himself stretches out his hands and throws himself on the ground to receive the punishment." The Indians were mercilessly flogged with strips of tapir hide sufficiently stout to cut them to pieces, and left to starve till they ate the maggots from their own wounds. They were suspended "with the feet scarcely touching the ground and the chain hauled taut, and left in this half-strangled position until life was almost extinct." Women held helpless in the stocks were publicly raped, men with smashed testicles were burned at the stake, and children had their brains dashed out.

Casement was particularly horrified by the most sadistic torturer, a Peruvian overseer called Armando Normand, who symbolized the connection between colonial exploitation, physical brutality and sexual domination. Normand had cut off the arms and then the legs of a captured chief "who preferred to suffer such a death to betraying the refuge of those who had fled" from their persecutors into the jungle. He also "put two Indian boys on a kitchen fire and roasted them alive. The skin peeled off and they were baked—but still alive." Normand's tortures of the Indians represented a kind of supreme evil that became possible only when man's basest and cruellest instincts, barely suppressed in Europe, were released under conditions of absolute power in the wilderness. Conrad had described the same conditions in *Heart of Darkness* which, like Casement's reports, attacked the hypocritical justification of colonialism by revealing the inherent savagery of civilized man.

In his Putumayo report, Casement raised questions about the psychology and morality of atrocities similar to those asked about Nazi extermination camps during the Nuremberg trials. "It may be wondered," Casement writes of the victims' passivity, "how numerous assemblages of men, not individually cowards, could be so coerced and dealt with by a very small band of oppressors." And he explains that there was no cohesion among the various tribes who had always fought against each other; they had poor arms, or sometimes none at all; and their chiefs and elders were taken from them and killed. But the military factors were less important than the psychological reasons. Suddenly, and for the first time in their lives, the helpless Indians were confronted with an overwhelming evil. Powerful foreigners appeared in their village, chained them together, and transported them to a strange and terrible place where they were tortured and forced to work as slaves under the most brutal conditions. If they resisted, entire villages were exterminated. It was the final solution to the problem of cheap labour.

Casement's second significant question concerned responsibility and guilt, for when confronted with their victims' accusations, the white men "only pleaded that these crimes had been committed under the direct orders of the superior agents of the Company, whom they were required to obey." An identical defence became familiar thirty-five years later at Nuremberg and when Eichmann stood in the glass booth in Jerusalem.

Casement had been in Africa for nearly twenty years when he began his investigations, and he was exhausted by long years of service in the tropics. He was racked by lumbago and arthritis, and malaria and dysentery had ruined his constitution. He had contracted skin diseases, and in the Putumayo he could scarcely walk from the eczema on both feet. He developed eye infections, and the insects buzzed around his sores and covered his body with large bites. He knew from painful experience how the constitution and character of the white man inevitably undergoes a subtle process of deterioration when he is compelled to live for extended periods of time among primitive races and in savage conditions, and the precise minutiae of his diaries reveal his morbid fascination with the atrocities. Malraux has described "The endless succession of days under the dusty firmament or the heavy leaden sky of the Congo, the tracks of invisible animals converging on the water points, the exodus of starving dogs under the empty sky, the time of day when every thought becomes a blank, the giant trees gloomily soaring up in the pre-historic world." This deterioration, accentuated by physical isolation and mental depression, Casement combatted with all the force in his power. For he had seen many men, the subjects of his investigation, revert to their ancestral nature and become thoroughly brutalized in mind, habit and temperament. His feelings in the Amazon were the terse but graphic: "Rain and packing up, very tired, very sick of everything." In 1911 Casement was knighted for his work, and two years later he retired from the Consular Service, his health permanently ruined.

Casement's long experience with colonial exploitation in the tropics made him particularly sensitive to England's subjugation of Ireland, and as the agitation about Irish independence was reaching its climax, he joined the fight for the oppressed people of his own country. The Home Rule Bill had been passed by a majority in the British Parliament, but the Ulstermen in the north, led by Sir Edward Carson, still insisted that only total exclusion would satisfy them, that if Ireland were not divided into two nations there would be civil war, and their jingoistic slogan—"Ulster will fight and Ulster will be right"—reverberated from Belfast.

In April 1914, 40,000 German rifles for the Ulster Volunteers were illegally landed at Larne, and when orders were given by Asquith's Liberal government to disarm this group, the British officers at Curragh, a military camp near Kildare, threatened to resign their commissions rather than fight the Orangemen. During this mutiny, for it was nothing less than that, the British government, for the first time since the revolution of 1688, had lost the allegiance of the Army and was helpless to enforce either the law of the land or their own declared policy in Ireland.

Ulster was bursting with German Mausers after the landing at Larne, and none of these rifles was ever surrendered. The importation of arms continued and increased, for on August 16th, after the outbreak of the War, the Arms Act was rescinded and the sole obstacle to the importation of weapons was eliminated. The vigilance of the police diminished and an uneasy truce settled over the land, but it was merely a postponement of the threat of bloodshed until the War was over.

While the Tory party, in their endeavour to achieve power in England, supported the Ulstermen, the Liberal party took no active steps to restrain their activities, which the Lord Chancellor called "grossly illegal and utterly unconstitutional." In July 1914 at Howth, in southern Ireland, the Nationalists landed 1,500 rifles to defend themselves against Ulster. And the British Army, which had refused to march against Larne, met the Nationalists at Bachelor's Walk in Dublin, fired into the unarmed crowd, killed three men, and wounded thirty-two others.

Despite his Ulster and Protestant background, Casement had been an Irish nationalist since boyhood. He had joined the Gaelic League in 1904, and under a pseudonym, had written articles supporting Irish independence while still in the service of the British government. But he revealed his astounding political naiveté in December 1913 when he addressed a Nationalist meeting in Cork and was foolish enough to call for three cheers for their political enemy, Sir Edward Carson. The angry crowd broke up the furniture and hurled it at him, and he barely escaped from injury.

Casement called the "nauseous fraud of Home Rule . . . a promissory note payable after death," and in July 1914 sailed to America to raise funds for the Nationalist cause. In late October, after the outbreak of the War which England had entered to protect Belgium, the oppressor of the Congo, Casement arrived in Norway with Adler Christensen, a

gaudily dressed and flagrant homosexual whom he had met in New
York. Casement's adventures in Norway are the first of many bizarre
events that marked the third and final phase of his extraordinary career.

When Casement left Christensen to conduct his business the Norwegian sailor revealed Casement's identity to the British Legation; but
he told his patron that he was suddenly accosted, taken to the Legation,
questioned by the British Minister, Findlay, given money, and told
to come back the following day. Casement encouraged him to return
to Findlay who, according to Christensen, quite bluntly suggested that
he should "knock Casement on the head" or help to get rid of him
in any other manner. Christensen said he was also asked to steal
Casement's letters and to lure him to a place on the North Sea where
a British warship could pick him up, in exchange for the protection of
the British government and five thousand pounds in gold. Despite
Christensen's betrayal, the British allowed Casement to leave Norway.
But the following month, when they realized his potential danger,
Findlay was actually authorized to pay Christensen five thousand pounds
for Casement's capture. Casement, blinded by his passion for the
Norwegian, never suspected his treachery; but he was outraged by the
sinister behaviour of the English and wrote a letter to the Foreign
Secretary "exposing" the plot against him.

Casement safely reached Germany in November 1914, in order to
enlist support for Irish independence, and remained there for a year and
a half. He had some initial success when he arranged the German-Irish
Treaty of December 1914 in which Germany recognized the State of
Ireland and agreed to help her win independence. Casement later
boasted: "I have committed Germany for all time to an Irish policy . . .
that, in all the centuries before, no other Power ever gave forth to any
Irishman." In order to create an Irish Army, all the Irish prisoners
of war were collected in Limburg Lahn camp, between Frankfurt and
Koblenz, and addressed by Casement who urged them to join the Irish
brigade to fight for Ireland. Despite the inducement of a distinctive green
uniform, better rations and living conditions, and return to Ireland
when circumstances allowed, only fifty out of 2,500 prisoners joined
the Brigade. For the captured Irish soldiers had been part of the
First Expeditionary Force, and were well-trained, disciplined and loyal
troops. Casement's campaign was met with derision, and he was frequently jeered, called a traitor and even physically assaulted. On one

occasion he was forced to defend himself with his umbrella and was protected from injury only by the intervention of his German guards.

When he failed to persuade the Irish prisoners and when the Germans discovered that Casement had no great following in Ireland, they lost confidence in him. He in turn became offended because the Berlin Foreign Office did not trust him sufficiently. Soon afterwards, Casement began to deteriorate, both physically and mentally. The old infirmities of his tropical career surfaced once again, he suffered severely from attacks of malaria, and in the summer of 1915 he had to be placed in a sanatorium for two months. He experienced great anxiety even there, and was visited by an agent of the secret police who asked for a military pass he did not have. He gave the agent his police identification card, but feared there might be a misunderstanding and that he would be taken to jail.

His dreams were frustrated, his contacts with the Irish prisoners of war had been a failure, he felt degraded by the condemnation of his former friends and colleagues in England, and by the universal suspicion which he inevitably endured in Germany, where his isolation was intensified by his inability to speak the language. Penniless, lonely, friendless and hunted, he sometimes broke down and vented his grief in an outburst of tears. By 1916 he was in a desperate state, and at times seemed to act like a madman.

Just at this point, when Casement felt hopeless, his fortunes suddenly changed. In the early part of the War the Germans believed that a rising in Ireland might be successful, but as they grew weaker and could not give it their full support, this belief began to fade. By 1916 they wished only to create a military diversion. During his year and a half in Germany Casement had repeatedly asked that arms and men be sent to Ireland, but English control of the sea made it virtually impossible to land foreign troops there. But when the Germans learned of the Irish plans for a rebellion on Easter Monday, April 24, 1916, they suddenly summoned Casement and offered to land him on the Irish coast with two other Irish soldiers in Germany, Captain Robert Monteith of the Irish Republican Army and Private Daniel Bailey, who had been recruited at Limburg Lahn camp.

Accordingly, on April 11th, the three Irishmen were driven to the War Office and given railway tickets for Wilhelmshaven. They were put on submarine U-20, which had sunk the *Lusitania* and steamed into the North Sea on schedule, but were forced to return to Heligoland because of an accident. They then boarded submarine U-19, and came round Shetland, through the British naval patrols, to the southwest coast of Ireland.

At the same time that Casement was sailing toward Tralee, the Germans sent another ship to assist the rebels, loaded with 20,000 Russian rifles of the 1905 pattern (whose ammunition could never be replaced in Ireland), captured during the war on the eastern front. But the German messages had been intercepted and their code deciphered, and on April 17th the British Admiralty received warning of the arms shipment and imminent rising. Four days later, on Good Friday, His Majesty's destroyer *Bluebell,* cruising off Tralee, sighted a suspicious ship flying the Norwegian ensign. When signalled for her destination, the ship replied she was the *Aud* of Bergen, bound for Genoa. She was then ordered to follow the *Bluebell* to harbour, and did so after a shot was fired across her bows. But the next morning, just outside of Queenstown, the *Aud* stopped her engine, and the crew blew up her hull and abandoned ship. The German crew of nineteen men and three officers lowered their boats, pulled toward the *Bluebell* and surrendered. Their ship sank almost immediately.

Like Casement's landing and the Easter rebellion itself, the *Aud*'s attempt to deliver arms was a hopeless failure. First, the time fixed for the landing was changed by the rebel leaders *after* the *Aud* had left Germany. Second, the *Aud* had no wireless equipment and so was unable to make contact with the Irish after the rendezvous had failed. Third, the Irish pilot who was to bring in the *Aud* was so confident she would not arrive before Sunday that he took no notice of the strange steamer and its flashing lights. Fourth, no preparations were made in Tralee for the receipt of the arms. And finally, the two Sinn Feiners who were sent from Dublin to meet the *Aud* had a fatal accident while motoring down to the coast that Good Friday night. The driver took a wrong turning in the dark and ran his car into the river at Puck, a few miles from the rendezvous. He left the car and was captured, but his three passengers were drowned. The Irish leaders at first thought Casement, Monteith and Bailey had been drowned; and Casement thought his two friends had perished with their driver while searching for him.

On the same day the *Aud* was captured, the U-19, after a rough nine-day voyage during which Casement was violently seasick and unable to sleep, approached as near as she could to the Irish coast, but the expected pilot ship again failed to appear. She therefore lowered the three men in a collapsible boat at about 1 a.m. The boat was swamped by the rough surf and overturned before it reached land, and the men had to wade ashore and then return several times for their equipment. The boat was too large to be destroyed or even hidden, and their small supply of arms, which were never used, were hastily and ineffectually buried in the sand. The men waited for daylight, and then Monteith and Bailey walked into Tralee to find help, leaving the exhausted Casement to rest.

On that Good Friday morning, an Irish farmer, John McCarthy, awoke in the dark at 2 a.m. and, for the first time in his life, walked along the shore to a holy well about a mile from his house in order to say his prayers. On the way back, as the tide was coming in at daybreak, he found the rowboat beached a few yards from the shore, a dagger in the boat, a large tin box with pistols and ammunition half-buried in the sand, and footprints all around. He went to summon a policeman and returned to find his small daughter playing with the pistols.

When Thomas Hearn of the Royal Irish Constabulary arrived, he searched the surrounding area and at 1.20 p.m. found Casement hiding on the beach in a place called McKenna's Fort. Hearn pointed his revolver at him and warned he would shoot if provoked. Casement said, "That's a nice way to treat an English traveller," and when asked what he was doing there replied, "By what authority do you ask this question? Am I bound to answer you?" When threatened with arrest under the Defence of the Realm Act, he said he was Richard Morten of Denham in Buckinghamshire and the author of *The Life of St. Brendon.* He claimed he had arrived in Dublin port at 8 o'clock that morning, but a first-class railway ticket from Berlin to Wilhelmshaven, dated April 12, 1916, was found in his coat pocket. Casement's bag contained a green Nationalist flag, a pair of field glasses, a flash signal lamp, nine hundred rounds of ammunition, a foreign map of Ireland, and some loose pages from a notebook which contained the notation: "11th of April, left Dublin for Wicklow. 12th of April, left Wicklow in Willie's yacht," the inveterate diarist's rather transparent way of describing his departure in Kaiser Wilhelm's submarine.

As Constable Hearn and Casement were leaving the Fort on their way to police headquarters, they passed a small boy in a pony and trap. The boy saw Casement tear up some papers and clumsily drop them behind his back, and after they had left, he went back, picked up the papers and brought them to the police. The torn papers were a type-written German code with a five-digit signal number opposite the sentences: "Await further instructions. Send agent at once. Railway communications have been stopped. Will send plan for next landing. Further ammunition needed. Further rifles needed. Send another ship. Send cannons. Send explosives."

In Tralee, when Casement was medically examined, he tested the doctor's political sympathies, identified himself, and asked the doctor to tell Austin Stack, the local Nationalist commander, to rescue him. The doctor delivered the message, but Stack refused to help Casement for fear of starting the rebellion prematurely, though a rescue at that time would have been quite easy.

Casement was then taken to London through Dublin, and when the train stopped at Killarney station, the head constable said, "Did you hear what happened to the two lads at Puck? They ran into the tide and were drowned." As the train left the station Casement began to sob and continued for some time. He then said, "I am sorry for those two men; they were good Irishmen. It was on my account they came over here." In Dublin he asked if he would be given a bed when he arrived in London; he had been up for nine nights and was exhausted.

He was first jailed in the Tower of London, "prey to the most distracting thoughts a man ever endured and of sorrow for what I knew to be taking place in Ireland." After two weeks imprisonment, "his clothes were filthy . . . his beard half-grown, his eyes red-rimmed and bloodshot, his arms, head and back swollen with insect bites from his verminous cell; he hesitated in speech and was unable to remember places and names . . . His boots were hanging round his ankles, he was collarless and had to hold up his trousers. No natural light penetrated his cell." He thought he was going to be shot.

But he was transferred to Brixton Prison and then charged at Bow Street Police Station, where he was relieved to find that his confederates had not been drowned, for Daniel Bailey had been captured the day after Casement was arrested and appeared in court with him. After the charge was made, he pointed to Bailey and said: "That man is innocent. I think the indictment is wrongly drawn against him. If it is within my power to provide a defence for the man, I wish him to be in every way as well defended as myself."

After a thorough investigation by Admiral Reginald Hall of Naval Intelligence and Inspector Basil Thomson of Scotland Yard (neither of whom, oddly enough, testified against him), Casement was brought to trial in the High Court of Justice in London on June 26, 1916 and charged with high treason. He was accused of adhering to the King's enemies elsewhere than in the King's realm, that is, in Germany, contrary to the Treason Act of 1351, passed in the reign of Edward III.

The constitution of the court was extremely peculiar and singularly inappropriate for a state trial in time of war, the first such charge against a knight for several hundred years. The Lord Chief Justice, Lord Reading, while holding the office of Attorney-General, had been deeply implicated in the Marconi scandal of 1912 and had admitted, but only after the first investigation, that he had improperly speculated in the company's shares. But this did not prevent his elevation to the high bench.

In 1903 Colonel Arthur Lynch, who was charged with adhering to the King's enemies outside the realm, was defended by Horace Avory, Lord Reading's associate justice, and prosecuted by Edward Carson. Colonel Lynch, an Irishman who had taken up arms against England in the South African War, joined the Boer forces, and fought in the field against the British Army, was the most recent precedent for Casement's trial. He was convicted of high treason and sentenced to death, but the sentence was subsequently commuted to life imprisonment, and he was pardoned after only a few months. He was elected to Parliament in 1907, and was serving in the House of Commons during Casement's trial. The recent clemency and present prosperity of Colonel Lynch, M.P., suggested that Casement should not be executed.

The Crown Counsel, Sir Frederick Smith, K.C., Attorney-General, who had defended Reading in a libel suit during the Marconi scandal, became notorious as "Galloper" Smith, Sir Edward Carson's second-in-command during the illegal gun-running at Larne, when Ulster threatened the tottering Liberal government with civil war. He had, in fact, *before* the War, committed a similar crime—the illegal landing of German arms in Ireland to be used against a hostile British government—that Casement was now being tried for *during* the War. This painful irony was obvious, but Smith, instead of remaining out of the case, deliberately led for the prosecution. Like Casement, he was tall, slender, muscular and attractive, but his icy character had none of Casement's gentleness and abstract idealism. He was a fierce political enemy of the prisoner, and brought considerable bias and personal animosity to the court. Smith's arrogance and intransigence, his cruel and devastating manner, was reflected in his penetrating, cold grey eyes and in his brutal chin. He expressed his brilliant pomposity and intellectual superiority in a characteristic vein of subtle and restrained invective.

Casement's defence counsel, Alexander Sullivan, K.C., was an Irishman with sharp, angular features, a furrowed forehead, and an immaculate moustache and goatee. Frail, and weary himself, he had a far weaker case than Smith, and was clearly no match for the overpowering rhetoric of the Attorney-General.

There were essentially two charges against Casement. First, that he endeavoured to persuade British subjects, British soldiers, and prisoners of war in Limburg Lahn camp to forsake their duty and fight against Britain. And second, that he landed on the coast of Ireland with arms and ammunition for use against Britain. In a privately published pamphlet, *A Discarded Defence of Roger Casement* (1922), Bernard Shaw suggested three possible lines of defence. Sullivan could contend, on the basis of Casement's diaries, that he was insane and unfit to stand trial; he could minimize the evidence, emphasize the positive aspects of Casement's conduct and plead for clemency because of his previous services and distinguished career; or, what Shaw considered most effective, he could argue that Casement be held as a prisoner of war and not tried as a traitor. But in the trial, Sullivan argued interminably on the grammatical as well as legal interpretation of the wording of the ancient Norman French Statute : that adhering to the King's enemies abroad did not constitute treason unless the offender was *in* the realm at the time of the offence. Casement did not testify on his own behalf, no witnesses were called for the defence, and Sullivan relied entirely on his own speech to the jury. The court ultimately decided that his interpretation was incorrect and that under the Statute a man could commit treason either inside the realm or, as in Casement's situation, outside the realm. Thus, the real political issue of the trial, whether the interests of Ireland were identical with England, and whether it was treason for an Irishman to support his *own* country, were buried by the legalistic quibbling about a technical point and never mentioned until Casement's speech *after* the verdict was delivered.

The jurors were a characteristic group of lower-middle-class Londoners, and the trial began with a humorous incident when some jurors with Irish names, who were challenged by the Crown, indignantly protested they were loyal Ulstermen and staunch supporters of Carson. Sir Frederick Smith opened for the prosecution with a characteristically dazzling speech. He explained the law of treason and the seriousness of the law; and recounted the notable consular career of the defendant with particular emphasis on the letter Casement wrote to the Foreign Secretary, Sir Edward Grey, when he received his knighthood :

I find it very hard to choose the words in which to make acknowledgment of the honour done me by the King . . . I would beg that my humble duty might be presented to His Majesty when you may do me the honour to convey to him my deep appreciation of the honour that he has been so graciously pleased to confer upon me.

Smith stressed Casement's "terms of gratitude, a little unusual, perhaps, in their warmth, and in the language almost of a courtier," in order to show what he thought was Casement's sudden swing from loyalty to treason.

Smith described Casement's ardent but ineffectual activities in Germany, and his efforts that deliberately exposed the hungry, and sometimes wounded prisoners, "his inferiors in education, age and knowledge of the world, to the penalties of high treason." He narrated the capture of the *Aud* and the landing and arrest of Casement, and claimed that "The prisoner, blinded by a hatred to this country, as malignant in quality as it was sudden in origin, has played a desperate hazard. He has played it and he has lost it. Today the forfeit is claimed."

The prosecution then called six Irish prisoners of war who had been addressed by Casement in the Limberg Lahn camp and who, with an almost incredible irony, had been exchanged for German prisoners and were thus able to provide the evidence that proved Casement's treason.

The next day Smith called John McCarthy, the farmer who discovered the boat; Constable Hearn, who found and arrested Casement; Martin Collins, the boy who retrieved the torn papers; Constable Riley, who described the damaging code; Sergeant Butler, who took Casement from Tralee to Dublin by train; the Signalman of the *Bluebell* who described the capture and scuttling of the *Aud*; a diver who recovered samples of the rifles, and a Russian colonel who identified them; and an English officer who identified the German maps of Ireland.

The defence counsel then presented his case—that the wording of this Statute of Treason did not apply to Casement—but his motion to quash the indictment was denied. Casement, not under oath and therefore not subject to cross-examination, was then allowed to correct several factual errors. He stated, "the knighthood was not in my power to refuse," for a refusal would inevitably have meant the resignation of his diplomatic post and the end of his usefulness to the Indians of the Peruvian Amazon. He insisted that he had never asked nor intended the Irish Brigade to fight for Germany, but only for Ireland; and he emphatically denied the insinuations that the prisoners' rations were reduced as punishment for not joining the Brigade, and that he had accepted money from Germany. Finally, he objected to Smith's allusion to the Easter rebellion, which occurred after (and despite) his capture. Though Casement took no part in the rebellion, it was nevertheless an important factor in his conviction.

Sullivan began his closing speech for the defence with a rather awkward appeal to the jury's sense of fair play. He re-emphasized the point that Casement recruited the Irish Brigade to fight with the Nationalists against the Ulster army, after the War was over. He maintained the Crown had not proved that the *Aud* and Casement's landing were connected, so that their case rested solely on the first (yet sufficient) charge of suborning the prisoners of war. When Sullivan attempted to discuss the pre-war gun-running in Ulster in order to explain and justify Casement's actions, he was interrupted by the Lord Chief Justice and told that no evidence of this had been given in court. Sullivan apologized abjectly ("I have been carried away too far, I am exceedingly sorry"), and rather incoherently attempted to continue his speech. He paused for a considerable time, and in one of the most dramatic moments of the trial, announced in surprisingly formal language, "I regret, my lord, to say that I have completely broken down."

The following day his junior counsel, Artemus Jones, concluded for the defence, but added little of substance to the case. He was dwarfed by the powerful closing speech of Frederick Smith, who summarized the argument of the defence and then tore it apart. He showed that the prisoner's intention was not, as had been stated, to land the Irish

Brigade *after* the War, but rather to land them in Ireland *during* the War, "in order to evoke there once again, the hideous spectre of disunion, disloyalty and armed insurrection." He convincingly argued that Casement went to Germany to recruit an Irish Brigade; that if the Brigade had landed in Ireland it would certainly have aided Britain's enemies; and that he landed in concert with the *Aud.*, Smith asserted that the Ulstermen "were never in his mind when he made these [recruiting] speeches, they never inspired the appeals he made . . . they are afterthoughts [invented] when it was necessary to exhume some defence." The most damaging piece of evidence was Casement's possession of the German code which, Smith emphasized, the prisoner intended to use "to assist the enemy in the war against our country." He forcefully concluded that "if these facts taken together : his journey to Germany, his speeches when in Germany, the inducements he held out to these soldiers, the freedom which he there enjoyed, the course which he pursued in Ireland, the messages which he contemplated as likely to take place between himself and the Germans, satisfy you of his guilt, you must give expression to that view in your verdict. . . . If you should come to the conclusion that the Crown has proved its case, however painful the duty, it is one from which you cannot, and you dare not, shrink. I have discharged my responsibility in this case; do you discharge yours."

The major point of dispute in the trial concerned Casement's intentions upon landing in Ireland. Though the prosecutor won his point, later commentators have insisted, incorrectly, that Casement landed in Ireland to stop the Easter rebellion. John Devoy, a contemporary Irish-American leader, wrote in his *Recollections* : "Casement went to stop the insurrection if he could, believing that a fight at the time must end in disaster and that it ought to be postponed to await a better opportunity." Eva Gore-Booth, the sister of Countess Markiewicz, believed this; and three Irish writers, Leon O'Brien, Terence White and Roger McHugh, in a recent book, *Leaders and Men,* have also maintained this view. But the Attorney-General won his case by denying this argument; Robert Monteith, a professional soldier and revolutionary who landed with Casement, escaped capture and was in the best position to judge Casement's intentions, denied that Casement landed to prevent the rising. And the most convincing evidence, which Casement himself wrote in the papers he attempted to send out of Pentonville Prison, is his rather romantic statement: "If I had been thirty-three instead of fifty-three, the arms would have been landed, the code would not have been found, and I should have freed Ireland, or died fighting at the head of my men."

The main purpose of Casement's activities during his years in Germany was to enlist German arms for Ireland, and his efforts were rewarded when Berlin decided to support the Easter rising. Casement was obviously disappointed that the Germans refused to send more substantial help— heavy arms, soldiers and especially officers—but was nevertheless eager to get a shipload of rifles and the assistance of a submarine. The *Aud* and the U-19 both worked to support the rebellion, and Casement rightly felt he would have a better chance of reaching Ireland by submarine. It was only *after* the *Aud* had sunk and he was captured that Casement realized the situation was hopeless (he had been in Germany and out of direct contact with Irish leaders), and tried to call off the rebellion. After his arrest, he asked to see the priest in Tralee and begged him, in order to avoid bloodshed, to get in touch with the Nationalist leader, John MacNeill, and urge him to cancel the rising. "Tell him I am a prisoner," Casement said, "and that the rebellion will be a dismal, hopeless failure, as the help they expect will not arrive." The final clause explains why, when in *Ireland,* not Germany, Casement thought the rebellion would fail.

Though MacNeill and the men in southern and rural Ireland listened to Casement and cancelled their military plans, his countermanding order was an important reason for the failure of the Easter rising. For leaders like Connally, Pearse and Plunkett, who were more concerned with the need for blood-sacrifice than for any military justification, went ahead with the rebellion in Dublin. Without national support the fighting in Dublin lasted for a week, killed and wounded three thousand men, wrecked the city, and incited English hatred of the Irish in general and Casement in particular. He was hanged, ironically, for the rebellion he tried—too late—to prevent.

After the conclusion of the Attorney-General's speech and the summing up of the Lord Chief Justice, the jury returned a verdict of guilty in fifty-five minutes. The convicted prisoner was then allowed to address the court, and his speech, delivered with great passion and conviction, surpassed even the dazzling oratory of Frederick Smith. One juryman said afterwards that he would not have voted Casement guilty if he had heard his speech before the verdict was delivered.

Casement began by denying the jurisdiction of the English court and claimed his right to be tried in an Irish court by an Irish jury. He challenged the validity of the ancient statute, dug up "from the dungeons and torture chambers of the Dark Ages . . . to take a man's life and limb for an exercise of conscience." And he condemned the formation of the Ulster Volunteer Movement in 1913 and justified the creation of the Nationalist Volunteers in opposition to them : when "the present Attorney-General asserted in a speech at Manchester [that] Nationalists would neither fight for Home Rule nor pay for it, it was our duty to show him that we knew how to do both . . . I saw no reason why Ireland should shed her blood in any cause but her own, and if that be treason beyond the seas I am not ashamed to avow it, or to answer for it here with my life." He quoted the Ulster slogan, "Mausers and Kaisers and any King you like," and stated, with a direct reference to Smith, "the difference between us was that the Unionist champions chose a path they felt would lead to the woolsack [symbol of the Lord Chancellor]; while I went a road I knew must lead to the dock. And the event proves we were both right. The difference between us was that my 'treason' was based on a ruthless sincerity that forced me to attempt in time and season to carry out in action what I said in word—whereas their treason lay in verbal indictments that they knew need never be made good in their bodies. And so, I am prouder to stand here today in the traitor's dock to answer this impeachment than to fill the place of my right honourable accusers."

Like Casement himself, the speech was impressive but ineffectual; and the traditional black caps were placed on the heads of the justices as the sentence of execution by hanging was pronounced. Lord Reading's cap slipped to a grotesque angle and Justice Horridge, who suffered a nervous twitch, seemed to be grimacing at the prisoner.

On July 17th and 18th, the defence argued the appeal on the same legal grounds—the wording of the ancient Statute—as in the trial, and the argument was again dismissed. Casement could still appeal to the House of Lords, but another ironic twist to the judicial proceedings was revealed by the Criminal Appeal Act, which stated that no appeal to the Lords could be lodged without the consent of the Attorney-General, in this case, the successful prosecutor. Smith later justified his refusal and said. "if I had given my fiat and the Lords had quashed the conviction on such a technicality, feeling against Casement was so strong that it might have brought the Government down."

Casement's last hope was a reprieve by the King on the recommend-ation of the Home Secretary, but this too was prevented by a startling discovery that added a strange and unexpected dimension to Casement's complex character. When he was brought to London after his arrest, the police found two trunks he had left in his old lodgings at 50 Ebury Street in Pimlico. When Inspector Thomson asked him to hand over the keys, Casement told him to break open the locks since there was nothing in them but some old clothes. In fact, the police found some personal black diaries for the years 1903, 1910 and 1911, the period of the Congo and the Amazon investigations, which recorded in frank, abundant and minute detail the homosexual activities of their political prisoner, and which radically changed the nature of the entire case.

Before the trial started, the prosecution suggested that the defence agree to produce the diaries in evidence, and that they cooperate in an attempt to obtain a verdict of guilty but insane. Sullivan, however, refused the offer: "I knew that it might save his life, but I finally decided that death was better than besmirching and dishonour." This decision was legally sound, for the diaries might have served as the basis of a separate action against Casement and would probably have destroyed his character without saving his life.

After Casement's conviction, extracts of the diaries were secretly cir-culated by Admiral Hall of Naval Intelligence, one of Casement's interrogators, among influential journalists, ambassadors, bishops and Members of Parliament, and were even shown to King George V. Before his appeal was decided, the newspapers publicized these private diaries, and one of them wrote: "It is common knowledge that Sir Roger Casement is a man with no sense of honour or decency. His written diaries are the monuments of a foul private life. He is a moral degenerate." The effect of this campaign was to extinguish the last remnants of public sympathy for Casement.

The passionate hatred of Casement was engendered even more by the "black" diaries than by the jingoistic patriotism and the hysteria of war. The sexual entries in the diaries occur nearly every day and are mixed in with descriptions of his daily work and social life, with obser-vations about the weather and natural surroundings, and with his extremely detailed and exact financial accounts. For Casement, a com-pulsive and repressed personality, the spending of money was closely related to the spending of sperm, and the former often financed the latter in remote places where bed and boy were easily available. Casement's entries vary from vaguely homosexual longing, "A lovely pilot-boy on board—young (15) and face like girl—with long lashes and peach cheeks," to gross physical descriptions. Considering the enormous amount of work and travelling Casement did, the tropical climate, his physical and mental exhaustion, and normal (or even abnormal) limits of desire and satiation ("3 lovers had and two others wanted"), it is obvious that most of the sexual entries were fantasies rather than actualities.

Casement constantly emphasizes the enormous and unreal size of the male genitals, passively observes other men's supposed erections, and imputes sexual desire to all the boys he observes. He writes, for example, of a soldier "with erection under white knickers—it was half way to knee! *fully one foot long*," and of a man who "had one below knees he could kiss." These entries suggest fears of his own inadequacy, for the sexual organs he describes are often twice as large as the usual size, always in a state of high excitement, and though erect, always *down* the leg toward the knee rather than characteristically upward.

Casement's passive observation is shown in entries like : "I hope almost at once to run across a good big one"; "Splendid testicles, no bush to speak of. Good wine needs no bush. Soft as silk and big and full"; and "one huge exposure, *red head and all*, and then Wicklow lad, knickers. 'His alright,' stiff." These are the admiring descriptions of a watcher, not an actor.

Finally, in an attempt to shed his guilt and to disguise the financial basis of his sexual encounters, Casement frequently projects his own desires on to those he observes : "Wanted it *awfully*. Literally begged for it" and "young dark boy, *huge*, wanted it awfully." Of course there must have been numerous physical relations as well : "Breathed and quick, enormous push. Loved mightily, to hilt deep"; and "He stripped almost and went in *furiously*. Awfully hard thrusts and turns and kisses too, and biting on ears and neck. Never more force shown." But even here, the somewhat masochistic emphasis is on the epic of superhuman physical performance, which shows a desire to distinguish and therefore remember the specific sexual event amidst the blur of anonymous adventures, and to experience in the retrospective recreation of the sexual encounter a sensation as great as the original excitement. It was emotion recollected in emotion.

The most convincing—and moving—entries are in the shameful and confessional ones : "Getting loveless men up . . . Mine *huge* and he pulled it out. Others came so I fled . . . And so again I have sacrificed love to fear . . . many stains on pants. I fear spoiled." When Colonel Sir Hector MacDonald was charged with homosexual practices in 1903 and shot himself in Paris on his way to face a court martial, Casement recorded : this is a most distressing case and "one that may awake the national mind to saner methods of curing a terrible disease than by criminal legislation."

Casement was a physically impressive and extremely virile-looking man, and until his diaries were seized no one had ever suspected he was a homosexual. His friends, and those who knew him best, never believed the accusations, and several books have been written to prove the diaries were forged by the English and that the homosexual entries were Casement's translation from the Spanish diaries of Armando Normand, which Casement had made as part of the evidence against the sadistic torturer. The forgery theory has now been completely disproved.

Casement's diaries are the only evidence that he was a homosexual, and though the Belgians mounted an intensive campaign to discredit him after his Congo investigation, they never accused him of sexual inversion. If he had sodomized as many boys as he claimed in his 1903 diary, they surely would have found out about it and used it against him. He was under constant surveillance in Germany, but there was no evidence of homosexuality during that period of his life. The diaries, then, are more fantastic than real : the projections of a guilty and repressed homosexual that attempted to satisfy his unachieved desires.

When the British Cabinet (of which, of course, the Attorney-General was a member) debated the question of a royal reprieve after Casement's appeal was dismissed, several of the more astute ministers, who were concerned about pro-Irish opinion in America, at that time a necessary and neutral ally, thought it best to follow the advice of the British ambassador in Washington : "It is far better to make Casement ridiculous than a martyr" and national hero, and to commute his sentence to life imprisonment. The Cabinet was evenly divided between clement and punitive factions (the latter strongly influenced by the diaries) when a decisive piece of evidence again appeared unexpectedly.

Casement had left a file of papers behind him in the courtroom, and these papers were returned to him—unread—in Pentonville Prison. Then Casement, with his customary yet incredible imprudence, sealed them up and asked the prison Governor to forward them to his solicitor. The Governor sent them instead to the Home Office for inspection, and the papers revealed that "the Irish Brigade might be employed in Egypt against British forces" if they could not be transported to Ireland. This was the decisive evidence that turned the Cabinet against Casement, despite political considerations.

After his appeal had been dismissed, Casement was officially de-knighted and unofficially defamed—it only remained to hang him. On August 3, 1916, brave and dignified in the presence of death, he was taken from the condemned cell at Pentonville Prison in London and walked up the stairs to the gallows. The heavy rope was ritualistically placed around his neck, his head was hooded, and the trap sprung with a hideous crash. In accordance with prison regulations, he was left hanging on the scaffold for a superfluous hour. Among the last words he wrote were: "Do not let me lie here in this dreadful place," but his relatives, who had loyally assisted him to the very end, were denied his body. Instead, his corpse was buried in a quicklime pit next to the gruesome murderer, Crippen. Some years later, in his epitaph of Casement, Yeats wrote: "The ghost of Roger Casement/Is beating on the door."

The ghost has never been laid to rest, and the violent controversy about his diaries, his character, his reputation and even his body has continued to the present time. T. E. Lawrence wanted to write Casement's biography but felt "the obstacle is that the Government refuse all access to those confiscated diaries . . . and without them there cannot be a life of him written." Inspector Thomson had said the diaries "could not be printed in any age or in any language," but they were published in 1959 in English. They remained in the secret possession of the Home Office until the year of their unauthorised publication, when they were finally made available to qualified scholars who immediately verified their authenticity. Despite his homosexuality, Casement was honoured as an Irish patriot. After prolonged and bitter negotiations, the Irish government eventually recovered his remains and he was given a solemn state funeral in Dublin in 1965.

There have been numerous books about Casement but his character and significance have never been satisfactorily explained. When asked about the German attitude toward him, Casement answered: "They could not understand me. They called me a dreamer." Casement was an emotional enthusiast who refused to see reality. He was idealistic and unselfish, and had considerable charm, but was high-strung and unstable, subject to periods of intense melancholy and self-pity, and to fits of hysterical weeping. His incredible lack of caution was more foolish than courageous, and he seemed doomed to leave a clear trail of incriminating evidence wherever he went.

Above all, Casement was an old-fashioned gentleman (he always commemorated Queen Victoria's birthday in his diary), intent on protecting and defending his honour even more than his life. During his interrogation he told Inspector Thomson: "I was not afraid to commit high treason . . . I face all the consequences. All I ask you to believe is that I have done nothing dishonourable." While drafting his final speech in the trial for his life, he made a sharp reference to the Attorney-General and then deleted it because "it might hurt his feelings." In his speech to the court he insisted that "a man, who in the newspapers is said to be just another Irish traitor, may be a gentleman." And after his conviction he affirmed: "I am already a dead man, but not yet a wholly dishonoured one."

In his last letter from the death cell to his closest friend, Richard Morten, Casement wrote:

> It is a strange, strange fate, and now as I stand face to face with death I feel just as if they were going to kill a boy. For I feel like a boy—and my hands are so free from blood and my heart always so compassionate and pitiful that I cannot comprehend how anyone wants to hang me.
>
> It is they—not I—who are traitors filled with a lust of blood, of hatred of their fellows.

In the hour of his death, Casement reverted in his imagination to his pre-adolescent boyhood, a period of parental love and sexual innocence. His repressive Ulster-Protestant background would never allow him to reconcile his sexual instincts with the demands of society. Casement hated himself for his desires but succumbed to them, and he punished himself by a compulsive search for death and an elaborate preparation for the consecration of martyrdom that ended only on the gallows.

He left Germany unbalanced and exhausted, and called the Irish landing "a policy of despair." When asked by the German submarine captain if he needed more clothes, he replied, "Only my shroud." After his arrest, when informed he would be charged with treason, he laconically answered, "I hope so"; and then added, "I don't care what happens to me. I have long gone past that." And before his execution, he was more passionate and self-assured than ever: "They want my death, nothing else will do. And, after all, it's a glorious death, to die for Ireland . . . I have felt this destiny on me since I was a little boy; it was inevitable; *every thing in my life has led up to it.*"

Casement's connection with Germany and the Irish independence movement led to a disastrous series of events that satisfied his unconscious yet overpowering death wish: his betrayal by the homosexual Christensen, Findlay's plot against him, the failure at Limburg Lahn camp, the collapse and hospitalization in Germany, the breakdown and return of the original submarine U-20, the rough and sleepless voyage, the deciphering of the German code, the capture of the *Aud*, the lack of a pilot boat in Tralee harbour, the swamped dinghy that could neither be hidden nor destroyed, the retention of the Wilhelmshaven railway ticket, the German code and his personal notebook, his immediate discovery by John McCarthy, the retrieval of the code by Martin Collins, the refusal of the local Nationalists to rescue him, and his fatal order to call off the rebellion. This bizarre combination of events shows Casement as a hopeless idealist, magnificently unprepared for all military and political realities, and landing in a spirit of self-sacrifice that was virtually suicidal.

These ironies continued during his arrest and trial. As with the ticket and the code, he consistently refused to take the most obvious precautions, and left his incriminating diaries in London when he went to enemy territory for treasonable purposes in time of war. They were discovered as soon as he was arrested. The composition of the court was strange: Avory (and Carson) involved in the Lynch trial, Reading smeared by the Marconi scandal, Smith deeply implicated in treasonable pre-war gun-running, and Sullivan, hopelessly ineffectual, arguing the weakest line of defence not only in the trial but also in the appeal, and eventually collapsing from nervous exhaustion. The release of the Irish prisoners by the Germans, the appeal to the House of Lords denied by the prosecuting attorney, the surreptitious circulation of the diaries, the campaign of defamation by the newspapers, the bloodthirsty hysteria of war, the capture of the incriminating prison papers, a weak and unprincipled Cabinet—all this brought Casement to the scaffold where he knew he must end. Anything less would have disappointed him.

Ironically, he was executed because the public was made to believe that homosexuals should be hanged for treason. He died, like most patriotic martyrs, more for his dreams than for his actions. His hanging was a moral as well as a political error, for if he had been, like Colonel Lynch, granted clemency and sentenced to life imprisonment, he surely would have been pardoned when political passions died down after the War, or at the very latest, when Ireland gained independence in 1922. Casement could have been an extremely valuable moderate leader in a country where many of the best men had been killed in rebellion or civil war, and he could have contributed to the settlement of the Irish problem, "the union of the shark with its prey," which remains bloody and insoluble even today.

Casement's two atrocity investigations helped to extinguish the cruel and exploitative colonialism in the Congo and the Amazon, and rank among the great humanitarian achievements of this century. Like his friend and contemporary Joseph Conrad, Casement was one of the first men to question the idea of progress, a dominant idea in Europe from the Renaissance to the Great War, and to reveal in documentary reality the savage degradation of the white man in the heart of darkness.

Casement's achievement in Ireland, despite his succession of over-whelming failures, was serious and substantial, for his deliberate martyrdom helped the Irish to forge the uncreated conscience of their race. His landing was reported by an Irish farmer, an Irish boy picked up the pieces of the code, he was arrested by an Irish constable, Irish prisoners of war testified against him in court, and he was betrayed by the Irishman who landed with him, for Bailey gave evidence in the pre-trial hearing and escaped prosecution himself. James Joyce was right when he said Ireland is a sow that devours her own farrow. Though the Irish helped convict Casement, the idea of a free Ireland was born during the Easter rising. When Casement realized his case was hopeless, he used his trial as a public forum to justify the rebellion and propagate the idea of Irish independence. He stands in the patriotic tradition of Wolfe Tone, who in 1796 attempted to overthrow British rule in Ireland with the help of the French Directory, and of Garibaldi, who in Casement's words, "went into the Navy of Piedmont to seduce the sailors from their allegiance, and was condemned to death as a traitor for that act."

Casement has found justification in history, and in his final speech, which has a striking relevance today, he asserted:

Ireland has seen her sons—aye, and her daughters too—suffer from generation to generation always for the same cause, meeting always the same fate, and always at the hands of the same power; and always a fresh generation has passed on to withstand the same oppression. . . . The cause that begets this indomitable persistency, the faculty of preserving through centuries of misery the remembrance of lost liberty, this surely is the noblest cause men ever strove for, ever lived for, ever died for. If this be the cause I stand here today indicted for, and convicted of sustaining, then I stand in a goodly company and a right noble succession. . . . An Empire that can only be held together by one section of its governing population perpetually holding down and sowing dissension among a smaller but none the less governing section, must have some canker at its heart, some ruin at its root.

Both Cunninghame Graham and Wilfred Blunt, lifelong friends of Ireland, wrote long letters about Casement; and though they came to quite different conclusions about him, they help to place his character and career in perspective. Like Casement, Graham had defended the rights of South American Indians, fought for Irish Home Rule, been imprisoned in Pentonville and was an amateur idealist, dominated more by his emotions than by his intellect. It is therefore surprising that Graham, who took a liberal position on almost all social and political questions, was extremely critical of Casement. In a letter of November 1928 to the journalist W. H. Nevinson, who had recently criticized Graham's attack on Casement in 1916, Graham wrote:

If ever there was a West Briton, till the last year of his life, it was Sir Roger Casement. His father was deputy grand master of the Orange Lodges of Armagh (I think). Sir Roger was a bitter, black Ulster Protestant, who, when Conrad and I knew him first, had no words, but of contempt for Irish Catholics. He passed his life away from Ireland, in the service of the country, that in the last year of his life, he called enemy. He enjoyed honours and a pension (both of which he deserved) from England. He was presumably a brave man, and did splendid work both in the Congo and on the Putumayo. The abnormality of his private life, which I hear from Conrad, from Englishmen who had known him in Paranagua and Rio de Janeiro, did not weigh with me in the least. As you say, we cannot hang all who have Casement's vice, and after all it is not a disease that is catching in the least.

As far as I know, he never opened his mouth during his long career in the British service, to say a word in favour of Ireland. He had, in effect, lived there but very little . . .

Had he been made British Consul-General in New York, most probably he would have been alive to-day. Many have told me that he considered himself unjustly treated in that respect, and hence his hatred of the British Empire.

This may or may not be true . . . who shall judge the heart, but it was common talk, long before his last adventure, i.e. when he first became a Nationalist, some fourteen months before his death.

His speech at his trial, to me, was nauseous, for it was palpably insincere. Ireland was not at war with England, he had done nothing to entitle him to call himself an Irish patriot. His very advent was forced upon him by the Germans, who were disgusted with his failure to engage Irish prisoners against England. He died like a brave man, and for that I respect him, as I respect the consistent courage that he showed throughout his life . . .

It is an outrage (in my opinion) to Owen Roe O'Neil, Tyrconnel, Wolfe Tone, Emmet, O'Connell, Parnell and Davitt, to place such a man as Sir Roger Casement in their ranks. These men (most of them) gave their lives for Ireland, but what did Casement do? Nothing as far as I can see. Peace to his ashes. May his bravery have washed out all his short-comings and his faults.

This letter is a rather poor justification of Graham's refusal to help Casement and shows that he was seriously misinformed about the Irish rebel. Graham maintains, like Frederick Smith, that Casement was more sympathetic to England than to Ireland "till the last year of his life," though we have seen that Casement had been an Irish nationalist since boyhood, had joined the Gaelic League, contributed to Irish charities, written articles supporting Irish independence and addressed nationalist meetings before the war. Graham repeats doubtful evidence about Casement's father who, in any case, died when Casement was six years old and had a very limited influence on his son. Though Casement was born an Ulster Protestant, he converted to Catholicism just before his execution. Though Graham claims to have heard rumours about Casement's homosexuality from Conrad and Englishmen in Brazil, there was absolutely no evidence that Casement was a homosexual until his diaries were discovered in 1916.

Though it is true that Casement "considered himself unjustly treated" by the Foreign Office (this led to his early retirement), he became an Irish nationalist for different reasons. It is extraordinary that Graham should state that Casement's final speech was "palpably insincere" for it created a tremendous impression in court and was made *after* his condemnation, when he had nothing more to lose. Rather than having his advent "forced upon him by the Germans," Casement went to Germany of his own free will after the war broke out, and spent a year and a half trying to convince the Germans to land in Ireland before they agreed to send him with rifles to strengthen the Easter rising. Though Graham asks, "what did Casement do" for Ireland?, he answers his own question. For Casement (unlike some of the patriots Graham mentions) gave his life for his country, and through his martyr-dom did more for Ireland than Graham ever did for Scotland. Though Graham respected Casement's courage, his bravery, at least for Graham (who presumed to "judge the heart"), did *not* "wash out all his short-comings and his faults." It is unfortunate that Graham's harsh and unsympathetic judgment of Casement was based predominantly on prejudice and ignorance.

Like Casement, Blunt moved from anti-colonialism to Irish nationa-lism; and in May 1914, before Casement sailed to America, he visited Blunt and inspired him with confidence. For Blunt recorded that he wished the Irish nationalist movement well and that "if anyone can manage it Casement seems to be the man. He is [like Blunt himself] well bred, well educated, altogether vigorous, and a good talker." Finch writes that Blunt "was touched to hear that Casement's chief reading after the trial was his 'Secret History Series' and to find at the end of a pencilled letter smuggled out of prison the message, 'give my love to Wilfred Blunt.'" Though Blunt's "Ballad of Sir Roger Casement" was never published, his letter to Casement's cousin, Gertrude Bannister, written just after Casement's conviction in 1916, is quoted in Blunt's biography:

I am gratified to know from you that you were able to convey to your kinsman Sir Roger Casement in his prison my deep feeling of sympathy with him and my unbounded admiration for his noble bearing at his trial and his magnificent apologia he spoke at its close. . . . In that noble speech he made a deliberate profession of his natural faith and chose to die, as how many other Irishmen have

died, for Ireland. . . . The Government would be glad to boast that he had weakened, that he had authorised our plea 'ad Misericordiam', and so rob him of his dignity of sacrifice and the glory of martyrdom....
[I have] sufficient knowledge of the past to be certain that the Irishmen shot as rebels and hanged today will be the accepted heroes of tomorrow, and that it is their judges and the English ministers who appointed those judges whose names will suffer most. Mr. Asquith also knows this well. He knows that, in Irish opinion, and in the world's opinion, there is no dishonour in your kinsman's action, whatever his legal crime of high treason may have been . . . I know that in his heart every Irishman worth his salt will hold your kinsman morally excused, and if he seals his treason with his blood or on the gallows, will revere him for all time to come. . . .
I have for him the deepest regard for the noble work he did as King's officer on the Congo and at Putumayo; and his courage today as rebel and splendour of his oratory in exposition of the rebel Irish cause, which moved me to tears of admiration as I read his speech worthy of the noblest of Plutarch's heroes, will remain with me as a source of pride that I have known him and esteemed him at his worth.

Blunt had quarrelled with Graham about Casement. Graham's letter reflects the contemporary opinion of Casement, but Blunt's statement that the executed rebels "will be the accepted heroes of tomorrow" has proved true. Like Shaw, Blunt admired Casement for his loyalty to Ireland rather than to the British Empire and believed he should have been treated not as a traitor but as a prisoner of war.

GABRIELE D'ANNUNZIO

(1863-1938)

I am a pig with wings.

D'ANNUNZIO

Gabriele D'Annunzio, poet, hero and cad, was the master of patriotic eroticism : the ability to convert sexual energy into political action. He was dominated by sensuality, nationalism and mythomania, and the egoism and excess of his books spilled over into his life. He was able to transform his romantic ideal into a political reality when he defied the Great Powers in 1919, captured the Adriatic town of Fiume and personally ruled it for sixteen months. But enchanted by his own theatrical rhetoric and trapped by his quest for self-glorification, he could not prevent the collapse of his most elaborate poetic creation.

D'Annunzio, a contemporary of Yeats, was born into a middle-class family of Pescara in 1863, three years after Garibaldi's Thousand landed in Sicily to spark the Italian Revolution. Don Francesco Paolo, the poet's father, gratified his lust with the whores he installed in his Villa del Fuoco at the edge of the town and slept with his bastard daughters when they reached puberty. In his autobiographical novel, *Il Trionfo della Morte* (1894), D'Annunzio provides a rare insight into his own character : "At the profoundest depths of his substance he bore the germs inherited from his father. He, the creature of thought and sentiment, had in his flesh the fatal heredity of that brutish being. But in him instinct had become a passion, and sensuality had assumed almost morbid forms."

D'Annunzio's biographers always emphasize the importance of his Abruzzi origins, but there is a considerable difference between the rugged and sometimes savage mountain villages of that region (which shares many characteristics of Verga's Sicily) and the prosaic port of Pescara, the provincial capital. The fact that he was born on the Adriatic coast was even more important, for nearly all his military and political adventures focused on what he called "the Gulf of Venice"; and it is significant that in a biographical note of 1894 he deliberately stated that he was born on board the brig *Irene* during a storm in the Adriatic Sea in 1864.

D'Annunzio, a lively and intelligent youth, was sent in 1874 to an excellent Jesuit school, Cicognini College in Prato near Florence, where he distinguished himself as a scholar and poet. His father privately published his "Ode a Re Umberto" in 1879, and later that year his precocious poetry, *Primo Vere*, written under the influence of Carducci, appeared with considerable acclaim. The following year he reported his own tragic death, the result of a fall from a runaway horse, which was mournfully published in the *Gazetta della Domenica,* and a requiem mass was celebrated in his Alma Mater before the truth was discovered.

In 1881 the young poet settled in Rome, where he spent the decade as a successful society journalist, and brought out another volume of poetry, *Canto Novo.* Two years later he married the daughter of the Duke of Gallese, a former French sergeant in the army of Napoleon III, who had married a noble widow and assumed the family title. When the Duke, understandably sensitive about his own humble origins, opposed the suit of the poor provincial writer, D'Annunzio abducted his daughter, Maria. Though the lovers were politely arrested at the railroad station in Florence and escorted back to Rome, they were eventually allowed to marry, and spent their honeymoon at the Villa del Fuoco, the site of his father's debauchery.

Shortly after his marriage D'Annunzio fought two duels and lost them both. In the first summer encounter a sabre gashed his scalp, the surgeon poured out an entire bottle of ferrous perchlorate in order to stop the bleeding, and this caustic chemical destroyed his capillary bulbs and left him totally bald. All accounts of the poet agree that he was extremely ugly. André Gide records that "His eye lacks kindness and affection; his voice is more cajoling than really caressing; his mouth less greedy than cruel." The French actress Simone describes his "deplorable colouring, his scanty hair, of washed-out colour. The protruding eyes, without eyelashes or eyebrows, had the bluish-green of soapy water. The pallid lips revealed funny little crenellated, unhealthy teeth. While his thick skin covered unequally a face which ended in a Valois beard." Sarah Bernhardt rather unkindly compares his eyes to little blobs of shit (*petit cacas*); and Walter Starkie calls him "a dwarf of a man, goggle-eyed and thick-lipped—truly sinister in his grotesque-ness like a tragic gargoyle."

Though only a hump was lacking to complete his bizarre figure, women found him irresistible. Isadora Duncan explains that "when he talks to one he loves he is transformed to the likeness of Phoebus Apollo himself, and he has won the love of some of the greatest and most beautiful women of the day." Nathalie Barney confirms that in 1914 "He was all the rage. The woman who had not slept with him became a laughing-stock." To reduce the number of women who assailed him in Venice he introduced the "hour of violence," and ladies arriving after ten o'clock became the object of any liberty the poet wished to take. Even the conservative Bernard Berenson reports that "in the presence of their husbands I have heard the most responsible women declare that should D'Annunzio try to make their conquest they would be unable to resist him."

The poet abandoned his wife and three young sons a few years after his marriage, and embarked on an energetic and exhausting series of public love affairs with wealthy, aristocratic and talented ladies, who frequently provided literary inspiration as well as sexual satisfaction. His liaison with Barbara Leoni provided the basis of *Il Piacere* (1889), Giuseppina Giorgi of *Forse Che Sì, Forse Che No* (1910) and Eleonora Duse of *Il Fuoco* (1900). There was a Contessa Maria Gravina whose husband brought a successful action for adultery; a Marchesa Alessandra Rudini who later became a nun and froze to death; another Marchesa Casati; a Principessa Nathalie Gobouloff, and numerous others. For D'Annunzio, like Don Giovanni, there were *"in Italia, mill'e tre."* During the war he sent passionate radiograms to Luisa Bàccara from his air-planes; in his boudoir at Gardone he hung the gloves forgotten by those ladies who had lost their heads; and at the very end of his life, writes his biographer Gatti, "One is stupefied by the contrast between the audacity of the propositions and the trembling handwriting."

D'Annunzio believed that "the soul is merely a lie of the flesh"; and a raw nucleus of semi-barbaric sensuality characterizes his art as well as his life. In his autobiographical *Faville di Maglio* (Sparks from the Hammer) he confesses, "Always something fleshly, something resembling a carnal violence, a mixture of atrocity and inebriation, accompanies the begetting of my brain"; and he remarks that the stories in *Il Libro delle Virgini* (1884) "should please the public for their air of sanctity combined with audaciousness. Its scenes alternate between the church and the brothel, between the odour of incense and the stink of decay." Though Henry James notices that a strange putrefaction arises from all D'Annunzio's concentrated beauty, and D. H. Lawrence criticizes him "as a sensationalist, nearly always in bad taste," he was an enormously popular writer. For as Lawrence explains with appropriate sexual imagery, the poet aroused and manipulated the deepest emotions of his audience by expressing their personal and political desires in violent yet high-flown language: "An Italian only cares about the emotion. It is the sensuous gratification he asks for. Which is why D'Annunzio is a god in Italy. He can control the current of blood with his words, and although much of what he says is bosh yet his hearer is satisfied, fulfilled."

D'Annunzio wrote plays as well as poetry and novels, and after a voyage to Greece in 1895 that inspired the poetry of *Maia* (1903), he linked his sexual and theatrical life with Eleonora Duse. Though she formed a company devoted exclusively to D'Annunzio's plays and became the outstanding interpreter of his works both in Europe and America, he betrayed her at the beginning as well as at the end of their "pact". *La Città Morta* (1896) was suggested by and written for Duse, but given to her rival Sarah Bernhardt to perform; and when he wished to get rid of Duse in 1904 he gave her part in his best play, *La Figlia di Iorio,* to Irma Grammatica.

During his Parisian period his spectacular play in French, *Le Martyre de Saint-Sébastien* (1911), had the scenery and costumes designed by Léon Bakst, the music composed by Claude Debussy and the title role played by the Russian dancer Ida Rubinstein; and he earned £4000 for the scenario of the film *Cabiria* (1914). His art was extremely eclectic and entire passages from writers as different as Flaubert, Nietzsche, Swinburne and Huysmans were incorporated into his own work. A witty "obituary notice" of 1904 satirizes his borrowings, aestheticism and obsessions :

Born at Pescara. Extremely precocious. Wrote, at the age of three, *The Loves of Oedipus and Jocasta.* At twelve, he was already known in all the elegant pastry-shops of Rome. At thirteen, committed first adultery and bought first *objet d'art.* To cover these expenses wrote 6 novels, 14 dramas, 3 "dreams", 2 opera librettos, 4 volumes of lyrics, 6 volumes of Praises, 2 volumes of songs of antique blood.

Although the material for these works belong to other authors, the subject of all is the same—incestuous adultery combined with mystic sadism.

After his brilliant success as a writer in the 1890s D'Annunzio was wealthy enough to indulge his taste for baronial life, and in 1898 he acquired Capponcina, a villa in Settignano outside Florence. Eleonora Duse was installed in a more modest house next door, and Bernard Berenson lived down the road in I Tatti. Besides La Duse, D'Annunzio had fifteen servants, ten horses (the favourites slept on oriental rugs), thirty greyhounds, and two hundred racing pigeons. He effortlessly spent ten times more than he earned and by 1910 had accumulated the fabulous debt of a million prewar lire (about $200,000). The desperate poet then signed a contract to make a lecture tour in South America and accepted an advance of 24,000 lire. But when the threats of his creditors became too menacing, he abandoned his innumerable possessions to the auctioneers and fled with a few trunks to France where Comte Robert de Montesquiou, the model for Huysmans' Des Esseintes and Proust's Charlus, introduced him into Parisian society and became his companion in dissipation.

D'Annunzio once told a friend, "I am better as a decorator and upholsterer than as a poet or novelist," and some literary critics would be inclined to agree with him. At Arcachon near Bordeaux where he set up his French establishment in 1910, he was able to satisfy his collecting mania and furnish his new villa almost from scratch with a 100,000 franc advance from his French publisher. His secretary Antongini describes how "the collection of Buddhas, started modestly with a diminutive ivory figure, in a short time swelled to such proportions that it overran the whole room. D'Annunzio rarely came home without a new Buddha under his arm." His purchases were so plentiful that when he moved from Arcachon to Venice in 1915, after a propaganda campaign that brought Italy into the war, his acquisitions weighed more than thirty tons and eight trucks were diverted from the western front to move them.

D'Annunzio exemplifies Malraux's observation that "In Mediterranean countries, politics is linked with the theatre." The poet was elected to parliament for the Abruzzi in 1897, at the height of his literary career, and revealed his self-indulgent motives in a letter to his publisher Treves :

I have just returned from an election tour, and my nostrils are still filled with a sour stench of humanity. The enterprise may seem foolish, and it is foreign to my art, contrary to my style of life; but, before judging my attitude, you must wait for the result to which my purpose is directed. Victory is assured. The world, my dear fellow, must realize that I am capable of everything.

D'Annunzio, who considered himself the "Member for Beauty," never visited his constituency and treated his political career as a monumental joke. During a parliamentary debate in 1900 the bored and exasperated poet rose from his reclining position on the extreme Right, walked around the Chamber to the extreme Left and dramatically announced, "As a man of intellect, I go from death to life. From Right to Left." But this *volta face* had nothing whatever to do with his political convictions, and he later explained that "For a single moment it pleased me to enter the lions' den, driven into it by my disgust for the other political parties!" Later that year he was defeated as a Left candidate for Florence; and his disillusionment with the mediocrity of what he called "a third-rate club" led to his nihilistic taste for a new order and a more autocratic form of government : "There is in our country only one possible political principle—that of tearing down the present political order. Whatever exists now amounts to nothing, it is only decay—death opposing life. We must destroy. One day you will see me in action on the streets".

D'Annunzio's aggressive imperialism, a regenerative solution to domestic decay, was stated as early as *L'Armata d'Italia* (1888) where he prophetically maintained that Italy "would be a great naval power or nothing at all." The final chorus of *La Nave* (1908), a drama of militant Italian Irredentism, represented the popular demand for the redemption of the Adriatic. His *Canzone d'Oltremare* (1912), written while in exile in France, passionately supported the Italian invasion of Libya (which was, ironically, condemned by the Socialist Mussolini, who was imprisoned for his views). And during that war D'Annunzio declared that "Africa is only the whetstone on which we Italians shall sharpen our sword for the supreme conquest of the unknown future."

D'Annunzio had had five extremely successful years in France when the Great War broke out, and he sympathized with the cause of the Latin race : "I glory in the fact that I am a Latin, and look upon everyone of different blood as a barbarian." On April 26, 1915 Italy, Britain and France signed the secret Treaty of London which gave Italy domination of the Adriatic in return for agreement to enter the war within one month. After committing Italy on paper the Prime Minister, Solandra, faced the formidable task of convincing the church, organized labour and a majority in parliament to change their policy and agree to Italian intervention. He therefore offered to liquidate the huge debts of the most famous Italian of the time and pay him handsomely if he would publicly espouse the cause to which he was personally committed. As Denis Mack Smith writes, "According to his own testimony, the government privately informed him about the Treaty of London before he left France, long before the parliamentary leaders knew the first thing about it, and the obvious conclusions may be drawn from the fact that the financial embarrassments now ceased for a while."

The stage was thus set for D'Annunzio's dramatic entrance into European politics and warfare, and his transformation from dandy to demagogue. On May 5th he came to Genoa with the two sons of Garibaldi, who had fought on the Argonne front, to speak at the unveiling of the monument to the Thousand, on the anniversary of Garibaldi's departure for the conquest of Sicily. Though D'Annunzio's magnificent rhetoric, a peculiar mixture of the grand and tawdry styles, is often indistinguishable from flatulence, the crowd of 20,000 democrats, freemasons, republicans, futurists, nationalists and revolutionaries supported Italian intervention, and they responded enthusiastically to the poet's philosophy of regeneration through bloodshed. "Italy shall be greater by conquest," he asserted, "purchasing territory not in shame but at the price of blood and glory." He predicted "The spirit of sacrifice will enter the roused nation, a precursor of the Italian spring"; and as Croce perceptively observed, by speaking of war in sexual terms as the passion of a supreme moment, "he reduced war in his country's cause to something not far removed from the transient thrill of a voluptuary's pleasure." For D'Annunzio, history was merely an extension of the self.

The poet continued his personal and patriotic propaganda in Rome, where he was greeted on May 12th by a crowd of 100,000 and contrasted Italy's past glory with its present decay: "No, we are not, we do not wish to be a museum, a hotel, a tourist spot, a horizon repainted in Prussian blue for international honeymoons, a delightful market where one buys and sells, swindles and cheats." His speeches, which combine the decadence of Wilde with the belligerence of Kipling, were a tremendous success, and Italy entered the war on May 25, 1915.

Though D'Annunzio was 52 at the time and had no military experience apart from his compulsory year of service in 1889–1890, he immediately enlisted as a lieutenant, and had a career of quite extraordinary heroism. Because of his fame he was given an independent command in all three services at once, conducted his daring campaigns from his headquarters in a Venetian *palazzo*, and fought a private war with unusual freedom and only a casual regard for his superior officers.

D'Annunzio first flew in 1909, he made the hero of *Forse Che Si* an aviator, and his greatest and most tragic exploits were in the air. On January 16, 1916, while returning from a combat flight, he was thrown against his machine-gun as his plane landed roughly and lost the sight of his right eye. He was forced to remain in bed and in the dark for several months, and during that time he composed one of his best books, *Notturno,* a sensitive celebration of war, by writing with large letters on single slips of paper (just as the half-blind Joyce would do with *Finnegans Wake*).

In October 1917 the Austrians, with the German troops released from the Russian front after the Revolution, launched the attack on Caporetto, broke the Italian line and hurled it back to the Piave. During that month D'Annunzio raided Veliki-Hribach (northeast of Venice) by air, was promoted to captain, and carried out four more raids on the Adriatic ports of Pola and Cattaro. In February 1918 he was on one of the three torpedo-boats that penetrated heavy marine defences, entered a sound near Fiume, sank an Austrian ship and returned safely. This expedition was celebrated by the poet in the *Beffa di Buccari* (Jest of Buccari), where he boasted that "In spite of the cowardice of the Austrian fleet the sailors have advanced with fire and sword to scare caution into its lurking-place."

D'Annunzio's most famous exploit was the flight from Treviso through the Alps and over Vienna where instead of bombs, he dropped his own propaganda pamphlets. The Italian offensive in the redemptive battle of Vittorio Veneto, on the October 24th anniversary of Caporetto, led to the surrender of Austria on November 4th. By the end of the war D'Annunzio had reached the rank of Lieutenant-Colonel after three promotions on the battlefield, been wounded several times, and received one gold medal, five silver medals, three Croix de Guerre, the Legion of Honour, the Cross of Savoy, and decorations from the Kings of England, Belgium and Montenegro. In Venice he had to register all his letters to prevent them from being taken as souvenirs. Ernest Hemingway, who fought at Caporetto and recorded his experiences in *A Farewell to Arms,* summarizes in a later novel D'Annunzio's paradoxical achievements and limitations: "writer, poet, national hero, phraser of the dialectic of Fascism, macabre egoist, aviator, commander, or rider, in the first of the fast torpedo attack boats, Lieutenant-Colonel of Infantry without knowing how to command a company, nor a platoon properly, the great, lovely writer of *Notturno* whom we respect, and jerk."

In January 1919 the Allied powers convened to draw up the peace treaties. John Maynard Keynes, one of the most perceptive critics of the Conference, reports that "Paris was a nightmare, and every one there was morbid. A sense of impending catastrophe overhung the frivolous scene; the futility and smallness of man before the great events confronting him; the mingled significance and unreality of the decisions; levity, blindness, insolence, confused cries from without—all the elements of ancient tragedy were there." Before and during the war the slogan of Italian Irredentism had been "Trentino and Trieste," and Fiume had rarely been mentioned; but with the disintegration of Austria the possession of that city became one of Italy's primary aspirations, and the Adriatic drama unfolded on the stages of Paris, Rome and Fiume.

By the Treaty of London Italy was to receive the south Tyrol to the crest of the Alps at the Brenner Pass; most of the Adriatic islands; northern Dalmatia, including Trieste and Pola; the Dodecanese Islands in the Aegean Sea, occupied since the Turkish War of 1911-12; and equitable compensation in East Africa and Asia Minor for the colonial expansion of Britain and France. America, who had been neutral in 1915, did not sign the Treaty; and the Ninth of Wilson's Fourteen Points was specifically directed against the Slavonic clause in the Treaty and asserted that "a readjustment of the frontier of Italy should be effected along clearly recognizable lines of nationality."

Because of high mountains the harbours of Dalmatia had no connection with the hinterland; and since Trieste and Pola were ceded to Italy by the Treaty, Fiume was left as a port for the trade of Yugoslavia and Hungary. Though the majority of the 50,000 people in Fiume were Italian, the town was surrounded by a Slavonic population, so that the Italian claim directly conflicted with the principles of the Conference.

According to Lloyd George, the Italian arguments expressed by Prime Minister Orlando (who referred to the fact that Croats and

Slovenes, unlike the Serbs, had fought *against* the Italians and then
shifted their allegiance from Vienna to Zagreb after the war), were that
"Italy had been struggling and often fighting for the best part of a
century to accomplish her destiny and obtain a livable frontier . . . and
now suddenly a State [Yugoslavia] which had hardly been heard of
before the War, some parts of which had been among the hardest fighters
against the Allies, seemed to have a monopoly of sympathies." The
Foreign Minister, Baron Sonnino (ignoring the fact that there had been
Russian and Serbian as well as Italian fronts against Austria), felt that
Italy had signed the Treaty with the Allies, had opposed the whole
strength of Austria, and had then been obstructed by America, who had
entered the war after Italy and attempted to impose principles in which
Sonnino did not believe. Italy also argued that if exceptions were
to be made to the principle of self-determination (which Keynes calls
"an ingenious formula for rearranging the balance of power in one's
own interest") "in favour of Great Britain (freedom of the seas and
colonies), and of France (the Saar, colonies), and in a host of other
cases (e.g. Poland, Czechoslovakia) it might appear somewhat strange
that strict 'justice' should be adhered to when it came to Italy." In fact,
Wilson had been logically inconsistent in conceding the Treaty frontier
at the Brenner, which placed a large number of German-speaking people
in Italy, and at the same time refusing to concede Fiume. "The battle
was thus inescapably joined," writes Harold Nicolson, "between a Secret
Treaty and the Fourteen Points, between imperialism and self-determination, between the old order and the new, between diplomatic con-
vention and the Sermon on the Mount. . . . The Italian problem thus
became the test case of the whole Conference."

The Fiume question occupied the Conference during April 1919, and
the Italian strategy, despite its glaring inconsistencies, was to hold
Britain and France to the Treaty while negotiating with Wilson about
Fiume. But Lloyd George records: "I found M. Clemenceau very
hostile. He said public opinion in France had been antagonised a good
deal by D'Annunzio's claim that Italy had won the war, and he was
by no means disposed to discuss favourably Italian claims anywhere. . . .
He was astonished that Italy, while claiming Dalmatia under the Treaty,
also claimed Fiume, which had been given to the Croats." Lloyd George
also reports that Wilson "threw himself into the contention between
Italy and Jugoslavia with an intensity which I had never seen him

display over any other difference of opinion in the framing of the Treaty. . . . There was a danger that when Italian emotionalism, which had been excited to a pitch of sizzling and sparking heat, came into contact with President Wilson's rigid and frigid idealism from outside, there might be an explosion which would break up the unity of the Allies." This explosion occurred when Wilson made an ill-advised public statement on April 23rd defending his "Fourteen Commandments," and Italy angrily withdrew from the Conference. Orlando's failure to achieve his objectives in Fiume caused his resignation on June 21st, and he was replaced by Nitti.

While the powers at Paris were arguing to an impasse D'Annunzio, who felt that "with the war finished I find myself in the blackest misery and have no desire to become a man of letters once again," was passionately advocating the annexation of Fiume. In numerous speeches and articles from June to September 1919, as well as in proclamations issued from airplanes that contained coarse yet lively abuse of Nitti and the Supreme Council, the poet made the settlement more difficult by exasperating Clemenceau and enraging Wilson. D'Annunzio was a voluptuary of words, and carried away by the dramatic moment, could not imagine the effect of his speeches—and actions—on anyone but his immediate audience.

The poet invoked historical arguments—Roman frontiers, Dantesque quotations, Venetian glory; and appealed to the pride of race, greatness of sacrifice, defiance of foreigners and invocation of the heroic dead. In January he "claimed Dalmatia as Italian 'by divine and human right' "; and on May 4th he asked, "Over there, on the roads of Istria and Dalmatia built by the Romans, can you not hear the rhythmic step of an army marching? The dead are moving more quickly than the living." On May 22nd Mussolini, whose newspaper *Popolo d'Italia* was (like D'Annunzio) anti-Marxist, anti-clerical, anti-government and anti-foreign, arrived in Fiume and in a public speech made a violent attack on the Paris Conference. Two days later in Rome D'Annunzio returned to a favourite, though rather distorted, theme : "How did we win the war? Alone, always alone, from year to year, with a faith that became stronger and stronger as the Allies reduced and suppressed the promised help. We remained alone to face a military empire of fifty-two million inhabitants now freed from the task of facing the enemy [Russia] in the East." The victories of Italy had been the victories of D'Annunzio.

Meanwhile in Fiume, where the National Council had declared the town Italian as early as October 1918, the Croat club was attacked and wrecked on the night of July 22nd. And a few days later, during riots provoked when a drunken French soldier tore an Italian cockade from the dress of a young woman, nine French soldiers (part of an Allied commission in temporary control of the city) were killed and fifty-eight wounded. With Fiume chaotic, the Italian government weak, the Conference impotent and Communist revolutions erupting in Russia, Hungary and Bavaria, conditions were nearly ideal for a quick *coup*.

D'Annunzio drew his main support from nationalists, unemployed officers and men, commercial interests in Venice and Trieste, and the seamen's union. The military command of Fiume was theoretically inter-allied but actually controlled by the Italians; and after the July riots the Allies agreed that a British force should take charge of the town on September 12th. To forestall this inconvenient change of command D'Annunzio, with *his* legendary Thousand men, marched from Ronchi near Monfalcone, about one hundred miles west of the town. He shrewdly calculated that neither the Italian or Allied troops would oppose the rebels, and after a brief but friendly colloquy with the Italian General Pittaluga, at noon on September 12th the poet made what he called his *"sacra entrata"* into Fiume. Despite his legions of mistresses this was his most famous penetration.

Fiume gave herself to Gabriele D'Annunzio as a passionate woman gives herself to her lover : it was a kind of political orgasm that emphasized the ineluctable connection between the poet's lust and power. D'Annunzio had reached the peak of his fame and wrote triumphantly to his supporter Mussolini : "I have risked all, I have given all, I have possessed all. I am master of Fiume—the territory itself, a part of the armistice line and the ships; and of the soldiers, who intend to obey no one but me. There is nothing that can be done against me. Nobody can tear me from here. I have Fiume; as long as I live I shall keep Fiume, unconditionally."

Giovanni Comisso, who arrived in Fiume with D'Annunzio, describes the ecstatic mood :

Fiume was a city of victory, of continuous victory celebration. The troops fraternized, and the city was full of beautiful girls, the shops and restaurants full of food and goods. . . . The inhabitants invited the Italian officers every evening to parties in their houses, lasting till dawn. Eating, drinking, dancing—this city with its irrepressible, overflowing vitality seemed Italy's prize for all our efforts. We soldiers felt we had earned it.

This hedonistic idealism, which recalled the glorious days of the *Risorgimento,* radiated throughout the peninsula : several generals and seven regular battalions deserted to Fiume, and by the end of September D'Annunzio had thousands of legionaries and four naval vessels. Osbert Sitwell, who visited and admired Fiume, observes that the *comandante's* men were, paradoxically, both the " 'spiritual grandchildren of Garibaldi', and the Futurists and professional soldiers who wanted to keep on fighting. . . . Thus, in a curious way, the poet united idealists with criminals, and joined those who love the past of Italy with those who hate it."

Fiume satisfied D'Annunzio's quest for grandeur, and he had endless opportunities to play the roles of a Renaissance *condottiere* and an adolescent Napoleon, a Byron and a Garibaldi all at once. He issued postage stamps with Latin mottoes below his own portrait, and many of the legionaries who swaggered through the streets with open shirts and daggers in their belts shaved their heads to resemble their *comandante.* The chaotic atmosphere was vaguely operatic and the soldiers, after dining on exotic food like crayfish and cherry-brandy, would organize amateur productions of the *maestro's* plays. The town seemed to sustain itself with fireworks, martial music, patriotic songs, processions and oratory; and it joyously celebrated its own saints' calendar : St. Gabriel's day as well as the anniversaries of the Vienna flight, the battle of Vittorio Veneto and the march from Ronchi.

The poet, who gave literary expression to the historical moment, addressed the crowd from the balcony of his palace every day and claimed to have established the first direct communication between the leader and his people since the age of Pericles. He proclaimed that the capture of Fiume was "the most beautiful deed attempted since that of the Thousand" and glorified the town that stood alone against the great powers :

An ideal grandeur transcends our thoughts and our acts, towering over us and the world. And all is fulfilled according to an imperious

harmony, through which misfortune and blows assume a necessary
creative vitality . . .
All the rebels of all the races will assemble under our sign . . .
And the crusade of all poor and impoverished nations—the new
crusade of all poor and free men—against usurping and predatory
nations, against the preying races and caste of usurers who yesterday
exploited the war that they might exploit the peace today, this noble
crusade will reestablish that true justice that a frozen maniac crucified
with fourteen nails.

Gabriele answered the menacing Fourteen Points of the paralysed President with his own "annunciation" : the eclectic though unique "Statute
of the Regency of Carnaro" (August 1920). The liberal and progressive
parts of the constitution of Fiume guranteed equality of men and
women, free speech and assembly, freedom of worship and inviolability
of domicile, and provided for compulsory education in hygienic buildings,
physical training, minimum wage laws, pensions for old age, and dis-
ability and unemployment insurance. Even music became a religious
and social institution and was "considered as a ritual language and the
exalter of the acts and works of life." But the constitution also contained
communistic clauses against private property and fascistic concepts of
the corporate state; and despite councils and cabinets, the *comandante*
"assumed all the political and military, legislative and executive powers."

The principal events that occurred in this nebulous nationalistic utopia
during the sixteen months of D'Annunzio's occupation were both impressive and bizarre. On September 20th he annexed Fiume to Italy. Later
that month he attempted to capture Trau on the Dalmatian coast near
Split, which was within the American armistice zone, but retreated when
given an ultimatum to withdraw in two hours. In October the crews
of two merchant ships mutinied on the high seas and sailed into Fiume
with their cargoes of arms and food. And Mussolini, who had failed to provide the promised support during the march from Ronchi but had, through
his newspaper, raised 400,000 lire for Fiume after the city was taken,
arrived to proclaim his support. On November 14th, to compensate
for the retreat at Trau, a thousand *arditi* (elite shock troops) landed
at Zara and seized the island as they had taken Fiume. And in January
the *arditi* kidnapped the Italian General Nigra, but soon returned him
in good condition. Inspired by such exploits, large numbers of officers

and men continued to desert from the Italian army, and by the end of the month the *comandante* had about 9,000 legionaries.

The capture of Fiume threatened to overthrow the government of Italy as well as the moral and practical authority of the Peace Conference. To appease the Allies, Nitti maintained the facade of an Italian blockade, but he allowed D'Annunzio to remain in Fiume in order to strengthen his bargaining position in Paris. Wilson remained adamant, even after his stroke in October 1919, and Lloyd George states that the President's "last spurt of will-power and energy at the Congress he spent on the futile endeavour first to cajole and then to bully a gifted but hysterical Italian poet out of Fiume. The more clumsily he cooed or the more loftily he preached, the more vehemently did D'Annunzio gesticulate and orate defiance inside Fiume."

D'Annunzio found it easier to seize than to rule Fiume, and a vital turning point occurred in March 1920 when the ruin of the port's trade, labour unrest and the threat of imminent bankruptcy and starvation caused serious discontent among the citizens of the town. This disillusionment was reflected in a hostile editorial in *Il Lavoratore* (Trieste):

> The legionaries of the dreamer continue to arrange for new carnival displays as though the financial chaos of Fiume, the ruinous unemployment prevailing, the food shortage and the black cloud of gloom hanging over the city were no concern of theirs. Military parades, divine service, sermons by Padre Giuliani, the consecration and presentation of flags, orations by the Supreme Command and by Grossich, reviews of the troops, etc. etc., are held *ad nauseam* . . . But who gives a thought to the civilian population of Fiume which endures the pangs of hunger and languishes in misery?

At the same time domestic conditions improved as Italy adjusted to a postwar state, and Fiume no longer threatened the internal stability of the country. And Nitti, now confident of the army's loyalty, began to seek a solution to the Adriatic question through direct negotiations with Yugoslavia. These changes spurred D'Annunzio toward the radical politics of his cabinet chief, Alceste De Ambris, and to more daring exploits.

In April 1920 the legionaries stole forty horses from the Italian army around Fiume, and when the General demanded their return, they rounded up decrepit nags, painted them in patriotic red, white and green, and delivered them to the troops at the border. More significantly,

D'Annunzio formed a corps of pirates, the *usocchi,* who raided the city, the countryside and the Adriatic for goods and cargoes. They captured the *Persia* bound for the Far East, as well as a steamer en route to Albania which yielded champagne, uniforms, munitions and millions of lire. Though himself "blockaded," the *comandante* inflicted considerable harm on Yugoslavia by raiding ships with goods bound for Zagreb and Belgrade.

Though Nitti made some progress, he failed to obtain a settlement by direct negotiations and resigned in May 1920. He was replaced as Prime Minister by Giolitti, who had led the country into the Libyan war, and in the *guazzabuglio* of Italian politics now reappeared to oppose D'Annunzio's nationalistic aspirations. Enthusiastic visits by the Futurist Marinetti and the inventor Marconi failed to revive Fiume, which suffered from administrative chaos and a severe shortage of food, and even Antongini admits that the town was about to collapse at the end of October 1920. The weakening of Fiume; the *de facto* occupation of Dalmatia; the pressure on the Yugoslavs by Britain and France, who wished to resolve the problem that had dragged on for a year and a half; the October plebiscite in the region of Klagenfurt where a majority of Slovenes voted for union with Austria, not with Yugoslavia; and the crushing defeat of Wilson's party in the presidential elections of November 1920, finally led Italy and Yugoslavia to sign the Treaty of Rapallo on November 12, 1920. This pact, which divided the former possessions of Austria and defined the frontiers of the two Adriatic nations, created the Free State of Fiume, gave Italy the territory between Villach and Fiume, the Istrian peninsula, Zara and four other Adriatic islands, and awarded the rest of Dalmatia to Yugoslavia.

D'Annunzio's response was characteristically farcical and impulsive. He sent an aviator to Rome to drop a chamberpot filled with carrots on parliament, seized the islands of Krk and Rab which had been assigned to Yugoslavia, and declared war on Italy. Rusinow states that after the Treaty of Rapallo

D'Annunzio's object (or dream) was Italian recognition of his regency of the Quarnaro, which would make it possible for D'Annunzio himself to become the Fiume Free State created at Rapallo, and he seems to have considered bargaining the Quarnaro islands held by his legionaries for this recognition. But he was a poor diplomat. He refused to recognize Caviglia [the General who replaced Pittaluga] as the sole plenipotentiary of the Italian government . . . and he sent to Rome . . . a myriad of irresponsible agents with whom the Italian government had no intention of treating. This procedure and the provocations and policies of his legionaries finally led the Italian government to tell Caviglia on December 10 that it found negotiating with D'Annunzio 'indecorous'.

The Treaty of Rapallo, which was very favourable to Italy, finally allowed the government to expel D'Annunzio from Fiume. This action was justified by General Caviglia who asserts: "more important than the liberation of Fiume was the need to place the Italian State in a position to carry out the promises given at Rapallo; it was even more necessary to suppress a centre of rebellion; above all, at that moment of extreme weakness when the Italian State was threatened by the destructive forces of varous political parties, it was necessary to restore faith in the army and navy." On December 21st four men were killed in a clash between the legionaries and the regular army, who repulsed a counter-attack on Christmas Day. The following day, on orders from General Caviglia, the cruiser *Andrea Doria* fired two shells on D'Annunzio's palace. As the citizens begged the *comandante* to give in and the legionaries pleaded for resistance, the poet, slightly wounded in the barrage, realized the futility of sacrificing the city and surrendered. The bitterly despondent D'Annunzio departed from Fiume on January 19th leaving "my dead, my sorrow and my victory," and in one of his most moving orations he mixed images of piety and putrefaction:

The drama of this world is a thing to frighten. The war has opened all graves, and not for the Resurrection. The war has opened the graves wherein lay buried all things accursed of old. The stench of decay pervades the land. The odour of rotting flesh fills the nostrils. Europe is a delta of a sewer that oozes away to the four points of the compass, and spreads pestilence everywhere. Who can nourish any ideals? What soldier can still think of his first thrills of heroism?

D'Annunzio saw himself as "a historical object of some value" and in 1921, when his almost demonic energy seemed finally exhausted, he refused to stand as a deputy for Trieste. But he bought—at a bargain price and with a substantial "loan" from the Banco di Roma—the valuable house and property in Gardone of a German art historian, Professor Thode, which had been requisitioned during the war. This house, along with his abundant possessions from Arcachon, formed the basis of the Vittoriale ("the house of victory") where D'Annunzio surrounded himself with the compensatory relics of his past exploits. During the last phase of his life in his Elba and Escorial, the poet shut out the world that had rejected him, recreated a new one in his own image and became the living embodiment of his relics.

D'Annunzio's novel *Il Fuoco* ends with the hero carrying the coffin of Richard Wagner in Venice; and this elegiac tribute suggests that the poet was continuing the grandiose tradition of the composer whom he resembled and imitated, for D'Annunzio represented the nationalistic Latin spirit just as Wagner had symbolized the Germanic. The character of both men was flawed by egoism, monomania and a streak of arrogance and cruelty that led to the ruthless exploitation of friends and admirers, the sordid treatment of their first wives, and a series of brutal and public love affairs. Both had a prodigious energy and a prolific output of eclectic art that combined neurotic, ecstatic, magnificent and bombastic elements. Both were frustrated in their political ambitions and enjoyed the patronage of potentates, Ludwig and Mussolini. Both accumulated enormous debts from which they escaped to another country, lived in incredible luxury surrounded by a court of worshippers, and became the curator and tenant of their own historical monument and mausoleum.

Like his hero Wagner (whose daughter had married Professor Thode and lived in the poet's *palazzo*), D'Annunzio found that a luxurious atmosphere was essential for his work. Wagner had said, "I cannot sleep on straw and drink bad whiskey. I must be coaxed in one way or another if my mind is to accomplish the terribly difficult task of creating a non-existing world. Before all, I must have *money*. But what is the good of hundreds where thousands are needed?" And his biographer Gutman records that as Wagner "grew older and excitement had to be whetted increasingly by artificial means, he surrounded himself with an ever more exotic decor of hangings, portieres, and counterpanes, about which he wandered in costumes that, by the time of *Parsifal,* approached the fetishistic". In the same fashion D'Annunzio remarked, "I am a creature of luxury, and the superfluous is as necessary to me as breathing. . . . Can it be that nowhere in this world there is an eccentric soul who will give me the few millions I require to work in peace?" And as early as 1886 he insisted on his need for "divans, precious fabrics, Persian carpets, Japanese plates, bronzes, ivories, trinkets, all those useless and beautiful things for which I have a deep and ruinous passion."

The Vittoriale (now a national monument) has a superb view of Lake Garda and is situated in an extensive park, sprinkled with pools and fountains, and filled with stone walls and commemorative pillars, marble arches and allegorical statues (including St. Francis with a pistol and holster) that anticipate the fascist architecture of Mussolini's buildings on Rhodes and Franco's Valley of the Fallen. The public part of the *palazzo* consists of military machinery: the high forecastle of the cruiser *Puglia,* once attacked during a raid on Split, which plunges through cypresses and roses and extends into the sky; the torpedo boat which raided the Austrian fleet in the bay of Buccari; the fragile biplane (suspended from the ceiling of the auditorium) that flew him over Vienna in 1918; and the long, open Fiat which drove him from Ronchi to Fiume. This material, along with some field artillery, an amphitheatre, the tomb of his wife and his own mausoleum are the more spectacular souvenirs of his extraordinary life. There is also a library of 30,000 volumes; and the D'Annunzio museum with its bloody banners and casts of Michelangelo's statues, manuscripts and first editions, photos, portraits, masks and busts, medals, ribbons and uniforms tailored in London, symbolic pomegranates and a bottle of Acqua Nunzia, a perfume derived from "the ancient recipe of nuns," which the poet invented and tried to sell, with small success, in 1908.

D'Annunzio's private residence (now closed to the public because of the danger of theft, breakage and suffocation), is infinitely more interesting and revealing. Though undoubtedly influenced by the phantasmagoric household of Des Esseintes, the decadent hero of Huysmans' novel *Against Nature* (1884) and by Wagner's Byzantine court at Wahnfried in Bayreuth, the Vittoriale is nevertheless a completely unique monument of narcissism in which everything reflects D'Annunzio and "represents a phase of my outlook, an aspect of my soul or a testimony to my enthusiasm."

The Vittoriale is a tasteless pasticcio, like Hearst's California castle St. Simeon. Its decor, which illustrates the aesthetic and militaristic phases of D'Annunzio's life, is a mixture of the Roxy Theatre in New

York and Hitler's house in Berchtesgaden. As Antongini writes, "Ancient patina-covered vases from Persia could be seen cheek by jowl with the poignard of an *ardito* of Fiume who died fighting. The small paunchy Buddha stood on guard over the screw of the airship of Da Pinedo, who flew the Atlantic; a rusted unexploded grenade postured between delicate amphorae full of rare perfume."

Like D'Annunzio himself, the rooms are small. They are super-embellished and over-decorated; the atmosphere is claustrophobic; the symbolism oppressive; the heating equatorial; the rooms perfumed and shaded to penumbra; the dominant colours lime-green and blood-red. Bibelots, curios, knick-knacks, bric-a-brac, souvenirs, mementoes, keep-sakes, baubles, *objets d'art* and *objets de vertu* create a chaotic impression of vulgar grandeur, sterile ritual and hermetic futility.

In this dream palace, more a depository than a residence, among his antiques, brocades, perfumes, jewellery, rugs, cushions, terracottas, dam-ask, cameos, enamels, coins, intaglios, reliefs, mottoes, jade and *japonaise-ries,* the poet wrote and loved. He spilled ink and he spilled sperm, just as he had once spilled blood. But sometimes his possessions were threat-ened by his amorous adventures, and he spoke with trepidation of one of his livelier mistresses : "She is a barbarous woman, sprung from one of the most savage of Mexican tribes. With her lynx-like bounds, she continually endangers all my precious objects which I have loved so much."

Like Des Esseintes (and modern film directors like Fellini), D'Annun-zio was granted an enormous amount of time and money to transform his private fantasies into an opulent reality. But his personal creation, his Wagnerian *Gesamtkunstwerk,* which once seemed so beautiful and heroic, is now merely vulgar and crude. This change in taste corresponds to the transformation of D'Annunzio's literary reputation, for the superman whom James Joyce thought had attained "the highest achieve-ment of the novel to date," now seems to be a rhetorical charlatan. He is tainted by the stigma of fascism in Italy and is nearly forgotten elsewhere.

All the prophetic theatrical machinery—the symbolism, mystique, style and farce—invented or exploited by D'Annunzio in Fiume was later adopted by Mussolini : the title of *Duce,* the Roman salute, the phrase *mare nostrum,* the black-shirted *arditi,* the song *Giovinezza* (Youth), the war cry "Eia, Eia, Alalà" (which the poet claimed was used by Aeneas at Troy), the oceanic orations from the open balcony, and especially the subversion of the Italian army and the sudden *coup.* Many legionaries later joined the fascist militia, the March on Rome in October 1922 was clearly inspired by the March on Fiume, and one of Mussolini's earliest aggressive acts was his repudiation of the Treaty of Rapallo and seizure of Fiume in September 1923. As MacBeth writes, D'Annunzio "was the last major writer who could use the Romantic ideal with its full political relevance before it went bad in the hands of the fascists."

D'Annunzio and Mussolini were like angry dwarfs shaking hands, and both tried to exploit each other for their own political advantage. Before Mussolini achieved power he manipulated the politically naive poet, whose popularity threatened his own position, by promising much and giving little, and by subtly undermining his opponent whenever he could. In August 1922 D'Annunzio mysteriously jumped or was pushed out of a window (he called it "the mystical fall of an exiled and mutilated archangel, but not the fall of a man") and was *hors de combat* at the crucial moment when his rival Mussolini was preparing his March on Rome. Once in power the dictator, who said "If you can't pull out a rotten tooth, you have to fill it with gold," kept the dilettante poet in safe seclusion with a huge pension, a promotion to brigadier-general, the title of Prince of Monte Nevoso (the mountain above Fiume), a luxurious National Edition of his works in forty-nine volumes and the Presidency of the Italian Academy. D'Annunzio, whom Lenin had called "the only real revolutionary in Italy," tamely remained under the supervision of a special police prefect while being enshrined as a respectable precursor to fascism, and fired off cannons from the deck of the *Puglia* for visiting dignitaries.

Mussolini quite accurately stated that "our temperaments are antithetical," for the *Duce* moved from Left-wing Socialism to Right-wing fascism while the *comandante,* who began as an autocrat and monarchist, moved steadily Left until, at Fiume, he embraced the radicalism of De Ambris and was feared as a revolutionary. D'Annunzio remained bitter about Mussolini's betrayal at Fiume, truthfully stated that fascism was completely alien to his inner life, and after the assassination of the Socialist Matteoti in 1924 startled Mussolini by declaring, "I am very sad about this fetid ruin." But he finally returned to his original and instinctive position on the Right, became pro-fascist after

1925, and enthusiastically supported the Abyssinian war (as he had the Libyan) in *Teneo te Africa* (1936). When the poet collapsed at his desk in 1938 Mussolini honoured him by sending the grandest sarcophagus from Dante's tomb to serve as his coffin. And when Hitler sent his para-troopers to rescue Mussolini from captivity and set up the short-lived Salò government on Lake Garda, the German officials assigned a villa in D'Annunzio's garden to the *Duce's* mistress, Clara Petacci.

Though Osbert Sitwell thought Fiume might develop "into an ideal land . . . [and] offer an escape from the normal European misery and vulgarity," historians who never experienced (and probably could never respond to) the enthusiasm of Fiume have been harsh in their judgments of D'Annunzio. Fiume had given herself to D'Annunzio as a woman gives herself to her lover, and Nitti (who exploited the advantages of the poet's occupation) believed that the *comandante* "treated Fiume just as he had treated his mistresses and left it exploited and exhausted. The cause had meant little to him, his own self-indulgence everything." Temperley regretted "It was a pity that an adventure not without gleams of idealism and courage had become at first extravagant and exuberant, and at last merely tedious and absurd." And Smith, who takes the darkest view, called Fiume "The first instance of international violence in postwar Europe. It prepared the way for fascism inside Italy, and outside it helped to destroy the mutual confidence between states."

These judgments help to place D'Annunzio in perspective by empha-sizing the aesthetic aspects of Fiume, the poet's egoistic sexual politics, his decline from idealism to farce and his proto-fascism. Though not actually a fascist, D'Annunzio was a political chameleon who always embraced the politics that were most advantageous to himself. Because of his extravagance and craving for luxury he succumbed to bribery before the war and after Fiume, and lived off the fascistic fat of the land.

Despite this opportunism, the capture of Fiume was conceived as a romantic expedition in the tradition of Garibaldi; and though the poet failed to harmonize his artistic talents with his political ambitions (the pragmatic Mussolini said that "D'Annunzio's political schemes showed fertile imagination but little realism"), he was able during a unique moment in history to gratify his personal fantasies with a poetic and political creation. His various careers—from Duse to *Duce*—as an aesthete, artist, lover, warrior, adventurer, *comandante* and relic represent a paradigm and critique of the modern Italian character, which "only cares for emotion." For after the seizure of Fiume, as much a *coup de théâtre* as a *coup d'état,* D'Annunzio could not transform the sexual *bella figura* of a dramatic moment, what Croce calls "the transient thrill of a voluptuary's pleasure," into a permanent and meaningful reality. But as E. M. Forster writes, "By the time he died he had a number of books to his credit, a still larger number of mistresses, and the city of Fiume. It is no small haul."

T. E. LAWRENCE

(1888-1935)

A great victory is a great danger. For human nature
it is more difficult to bear than defeat.

NIETZSCHE, *Untimely Meditations*

T. E. Lawrence—archaeologist, linguist, soldier, strategist, politician,
writer and inventor—represents a superb conjunction between hero
and history. He applied his intelligence to war and politics with supreme
success, organized and led a victorious Arab army against the Turks in
the Great War, survived to write the history of his own campaigns, and
helped to establish the Hashemite kingdoms of Iraq and Transjordan.

Lawrence had a Dionysian personality—morbid, masochistic, patho-
logical; charismatic, passionate, possessed—and Nietzsche's ideas about
transmuting suffering into knowledge, creative agony, self-overcoming
and the supremacy of the will to power dominated his thought and
action. In "The Will to Power as Art," a section of his final book,
Nietzsche describes the three phases of the power of art, "the great
stimulant to life," which correspond very closely to the three phases of
Lawrence's life : intellectual, warrior, agonist.

> Art as the *redemption of the man of knowledge*—of those who see
> the terrifying and questionable character of existence, who want to see
> it, the men of tragic knowledge.
> Art as the *redemption of the man of action*—of those who not only
> see the terrifying and questionable character of existence but live it,
> want to live it, the tragic-warlike man, the hero.
> Art as the *redemption of the sufferer*—as the way to states in which
> suffering is willed, transfigured, deified, where suffering is a form of
> great delight.

During the first phase of his life, as intellectual, Lawrence was intensely idealistic. During his second phase as a warrior, he used his heroic will to power to translate his ideals into action. But during the war his will was pushed to the extreme limits of endurance and was finally broken by torture. This breakdown led to Lawrence's final phase as agonist, not only in the war but also in his self-imposed penance in the ranks of the R.A.F., where he spent the last thirteen years of his life serving machines and trying to become like one. Lawrence saw war as an expression of individual heroism and was too sensitive to withstand its brutality; he thought politics should be conducted honourably and was too idealistic to accept its lack of principle. Though Lawrence achieved his military and political ambitions, his idealism and will were destroyed in the course of his ironic victory, and he retreated into nihilism and despair.

Lawrence's mother, Sarah Maden, had a profound influence on his life. She was an illegitimate child, brought up under the rigorous regimen of Presbyterian puritanism which she powerfully impressed on her son. She was sent to Ireland as a young woman to be a maid in the house of Sir Thomas Chapman, Lawrence's father, who had long been married to an attractive, unsympathetic and unbalanced woman, who had borne him four daughters. Though passion momentarily overcame repression when Sarah ran off with Sir Thomas (who could never obtain a divorce), she soon reverted to an even more fanatical religion as the "sinful" birth of her five sons repeated her mother's "crime" and intensified her own fears of eternal damnation. In 1922, when she was 61 years old, the strong-willed Sarah Lawrence continued her penance, joined her eldest son Bob, and became a missionary in China. She died in 1959 at the age of 98.

Sir Thomas changed his family name to Lawrence, and Thomas Edward, the second of five sons, was born in Tremadoc, North Wales, on Napoleon's birthday, August 15, 1888. In an essay written after her son's death, Sarah Lawrence describes how (in an anxious attempt to preserve their guilty secret) the family frequently moved from place to place during the first eight years of Lawrence's extremely unsettled childhood. "When he was 13 months old we left Wales and took a house at Kirkcudbright in the south of Scotland where we remained till he was nearly three. . . . We went to the Isle of Man for a few weeks, where he had his third birthday; then on to Jersey for three months, and in December 1891 we went to Dinard. . . . In the spring of 1894 we left

France and took a small place in Langley on the borders of the New Forest. . . . When he was 8 years old we moved to Oxford, September 1896." Lawrence attended Oxford High School from that year until 1907.

In a letter to Bernard Shaw's wife, Charlotte, who was 65 when she first met Lawrence in 1922, the year his mother left for China, Lawrence made some extraordinary revelations about his family and himself :

> My mother was brought up as a child of sin in the Island of Skye by a bible-thinking Presbyterian, then a nurse maid, then "guilty" (in her judgment) of taking my father from his wife. . . . My father was on the large scale, tolerant, experienced, grand, rash, humoursome . . . a spendthrift, a sportsman, and a hard rider and drinker. . . . She was wholly wrapped up in my father . . . whom she kept as her trophy of power. Also she was a fanatical housewife. . . . To justify herself, she remodelled my father, making him a teetotaler. . . . They thought always that they were living in sin, and that we would someday find it out. Whereas I knew it before I was ten, and they never told me; till after my father's death something I said showed mother that I knew, and didn't care a straw. . . . I have a terror of her knowing anything about my feelings, or convictions, or way of life. If she knew they would be damaged : violated : no longer mine. You see, she would not hesitate to understand them : and I do not understand them, and do not want to. . . . Knowledge of her will prevent my ever making any woman a mother, and the cause of children. I think she suspects this. . . . They should not have borne children.

This remarkable letter from the normally reticent Lawrence reveals a number of crucial points. It is clear that the withdrawn and ascetic Lawrence inherited few of his father's grand characteristics and a great many of his mother's. After considerable conflict, the mother totally dominated and completely transformed the father, who was a hopeless drunkard, and her sons also became trophies of her authoritarian power. Her fanaticism manifested itself not only in religion but also in extremes of cleanliness and discipline, and she often usurped the father's role and punished her sons with humiliating whippings on their bare bodies.

Lawrence tried to escape from his parents' discord by moving to a small cottage in the garden, and he joined the artillery in 1906 because of trouble at home and did eight months service before being bought out.

Sarah Lawrence proudly records that her son "was for many years a constant worshipper at St. Aldate's Church and taught in the Sunday School there twice every Sunday. He had the great privilege of Canon A. M. W. Christopher's gospel teaching from his early years till he left Oxford in 1910." Lawrence's constant worship was undoubtedly enforced by his domineering mother, and his break from religion in 1910 was clearly an attempt to free himself of her influence. When serving in the ranks Lawrence submitted to every form of harsh discipline, but he always refused to attend church parade.

Lawrence grew up in an atmosphere of overwhelming sin and guilt, and discovered the source of this guilt just as he entered the vulnerable period of adolescence. His statement that he "didn't care a straw" is a rather unconvincing whistling in the dark. It is difficult to assess (but easy to underestimate) the influence of Lawrence's illegitimacy on his personality, but it must have intensified, if not determined, his odd combination of shy reserve and provocative aggressiveness, his alienation and isolation, and his sense of shame and degradation.

The letter to Charlotte Shaw also shows that Lawrence felt his mother threateningly close to him, and because she was able to pierce the core of his inner self, he had to erect a barrier of secrecy to protect himself from her. (The lengthy descriptions of the castles in the *Home Letters* are an attempt to maintain a formal distance from his mother.) Because of their strong similarity, Lawrence developed a keen insight into his mother's puritanical shame and guilt. He asked the astonished Arabs "how they could look with pleasure on children, embodied proofs of their consummated lust?", and admired the Greek epitaph : "Here I lie of Tarsus/Never having married, and would that my father had not." But Lawrence's insight did not liberate him from his mother's feelings : it led him to revulsion and disgust for the sexual aspect of women and to a desire for sexual relations with men.

The strange and enigmatic personality of Jonathan Swift provides a suggestive analogy to the divided Lawrence. Swift, a posthumous child and Lawrence, an illegitimate one, had radically disturbed and covertly hostile relationships with their parents. Both had a proud and anguished character, a horror of the physical side of life, a compulsive cleanliness and a perverse sexual attitude as well as a considerable achievement in literature and politics, a number of brilliant and powerful friends, a soaring ambition briefly gratified and permanently disappointed. And both spent the last part of their lives in obscurity, amidst humble and adoring mediocrities.

Lawrence was very short (about 5' 4") and slight, with fair hair and brilliant blue eyes which, an Arab woman once told him, looked "like the sky shining through the eye-sockets of an empty skull." Despite his large forehead and long jaw, he retained a shy, boyish air throughout his life; and he never lost his taste for practical jokes, exotic clothing and unconventional behaviour.

As a boy Lawrence developed a passionate desire for a knowledge of the past and became absorbed in medieval heraldry, monumental brasses, church architecture, ruins, castles, arms and armour. He read history at Jesus College, Oxford, from 1907 to 1910; went on solitary bicycling tours of French castles in the summer holidays of 1906–1908; and became an expert with a camera and a revolver.

To prepare himself for his undergraduate thesis on the medieval military architecture of the Middle East, Lawrence decided to inspect all the castles in Syria. His initial visit to the East was inspired by Charles Doughty, who had wandered in Arabia for two years during 1876–1878, spent ten years composing *Travels in Arabia Deserta*, and published the book in 1888, the year Lawrence was born. Before he set out on the first of many journeys Lawrence wrote to the sage for advice and encouragement. Doughty cautioned Lawrence, "Long daily marches on foot a prudent man who knows the country would I think consider out of the question . . . I should dissuade a friend from such a voyage, which is too likely to be most wearisome, hazardous to health and even disappointing." The impetuous Lawrence took this warning as a challenge and travelled a thousand miles on foot through Syria during the intense heat of high summer. Doughty's advice was sound, for on this journey in 1909 Lawrence was attacked by Kurds who beat and robbed him, molested him sexually and left him for dead. But Lawrence was nursed back to health, and the following year wrote his first class honours thesis, *Crusader Castles* (published in 1936), which contradicted the accepted theory and definitively concluded that "the Crusading architects were for many years copyists of the Western builders."

Through the recommendation of the archaeologist David Hogarth, the Keeper of the Ashmolean Museum in Oxford, who became the first in Lawrence's series of surrogate fathers (he was succeeded by Allenby,

Churchill and Air Vice-Marshal Trenchard), Lawrence joined the excavations at Carchemish on the Euphrates River in northeast Syria and spent the three happiest years of his life working there from 1911 to 1914.

At the Carchemish dig the 23-year-old Lawrence met the 14-year-old Sheik Ahmed or Dahoum (he was known by both names) who had Arab and Hittite blood. Leonard Woolley, Lawrence's fellow archaeologist, reproduces some photographs of the lovely but "not particularly intelligent" boy in *Dead Towns and Living Men,* and gives the most complete picture of him. Dahoum was

> beautifully built and remarkably handsome. Lawrence was devoted to him. The Arabs were tolerantly scandalized by the friendship, especially when in 1913 Lawrence, stopping in the house after the dig was over, had Dahoum to live with him and got him to pose as a model for a queer crouching figure which he carved in the soft local limestone and set up on the edge of the house roof; to make an image was bad enough in its way, but to portray a naked figure was proof to them of evil of another sort. The scandal about Lawrence was widely spread and firmly believed. . . . He knew quite well what the Arabs said about himself and Dahoum and so far from resenting it was amused, and I think that he courted misunderstanding rather than tried to avoid it.

Lawrence formed a blood-brotherhood with him, took him on a visit to England in 1913, and dedicated *Seven Pillars of Wisdom* to Sheik Ahmed ("S.A."), who inspired his leadership of the Arab Revolt:

> I loved you, so I drew these tides of men into my hands
>   and wrote my will across the sky in stars
> To earn you, Freedom, the seven pillared worthy house,
>   that your eyes might be shining for me
>   When we came.

And in the intense and poetic Epilogue to the book Lawrence again refers to Dahoum, who died of typhus behind Turkish lines in 1918, before the capture of Damascus:

> The strongest motive throughout had been a personal one, not mentioned here, but present to me, I think, every hour of these two years. Active pains and joys might fling up, like towers, among my days:

but, refluent as air, this hidden urge re-formed, to be the persisting element of life, till near the end. It was dead, before we reached Damascus.

Lawrence's approach to the Arab Revolt, an ambitious and long-nurtured quest for national freedom, was intellectual, practical and idealistic. His pursuit of the past was at first academic and archaeological, and the chivalric code of the Middle Ages drew him to Gothic churches and crusader castles. He was especially attracted to Richard the Lion-Hearted, the greatest English crusader, and as early as 1907 he wrote to his mother, "Richard I must have been a far greater man than we usually consider him : he must have been a great strategist and a great engineer, as well as a great man-at-arms." In 1911 Lawrence planned a monumental book on the Crusades, and once in Arabia he imagined that *his* crusade would boast the union of the two great warrior kings : Richard (Lawrence) and Saladin (Feisal). And Lawrence's description of the Emir Feisal's character is remarkably close to his own : "A popular idol, and ambitious; full of dreams, and the capacity to realize them, with keen personal insight."

Lawrence spent only seven months in England in the years between December 1910 and August 1914, and his considerable practical experience in the Middle East transformed the man of knowledge into the man of action and prepared him for the leadership of the Arab Revolt. He learned Arabic, expertly commanded the large number of workers at Carchemish and earned the admiration of their foreman, Sheik Hamoudi : "Tell them in England of what I say. Of manhood the man, in freedom free; a mind without equal; I can see no flaw in him." Lawrence toughened himself physically and in 1912 went on foot from Carchemish to Beredjik and back within sixteen hours, a "great feat" that no one had ever done before. He had walked across most of Syria before the war; studied the campaigns of Mohammed, Saladin, Napoleon and the Egyptian general Ibrahim Pasha as well as of Hannibal and Belisarius; and felt that "these modern wars of large armies and long-range weapons are quite unfitted for the historic battlefields." Liddell Hart, the foremost authority on military history, places Lawrence with the Great Captains and believes that he "was more deeply steeped in knowledge of war than any of the generals of the [Great] war."

But Lawrence's early experience was not confined to the study of military history and theory. In January and February 1914, Lawrence and Woolley were sent by Lord Kitchener to conduct an archaeological expedition in Sinai as a cover for a secret military survey of the peninsula; and the scholarly record of their investigations was published as *The Wilderness of Zin* (1915). When the war broke out Lawrence joined the Arab Bureau under his friend and mentor David Hogarth, and worked on military intelligence in Cairo until October 1916. During these years he undertook significant secret missions. The Senussi tribe of the Libyan desert responded to a Turkish proclamation of a *jihad* and under Jaafar Pasha (who was captured and later fought on Lawrence's side) and other capable Turkish army officers, had some success on the Egyptian frontier. According to Robert Graves, Lawrence visited the Senussi desert "to discover the whereabouts of British prisoners captured by the hostile Arabs there." Graves continues that "He was also sent to Athens to get contact with the Levant group of the British Secret Service, whose agent in Egypt he was for a time until the work grew too important for an officer of his low rank to perform."

Early in 1916, through the War Office and the British Military Attaché in Russia, Lawrence put the Grand Duke Nicholas in touch with certain disaffected Arab officers in the Turkish city of Erzerum, which was then captured by the Russians. (John Buchan's *Greenmantle* is a fictional account of this.) The War Office thought Lawrence could perform a similar service in Mesopotamia for the 10,000 man British garrison under General Townshend at Kut, which had been besieged by the Turks since the previous winter and was threatened with anni-hilation. In April 1916 Lawrence was authorized to offer the Turkish commander two million pounds to free the garrison. Unfortunately, this offer was disdainfully refused and Townshend was forced to surrender unconditionally on April 28th.

In *Seven Pillars* Lawrence speaks of himself as an "armed prophet" on a "return pilgrimage", and these two concepts fused in his "armed pilgrimage" to Damascus. Lawrence wanted to free Arabia from the Turks not only to provide a fitting monument to the memory of Dahoum but also, as he narrates in the Epilogue, to satisfy his patriotism, his intellectual curiosity and his historical ambition.

Next in force had been a pugnacious wish to win the war: yoked to the conviction that without Arab help England could not pay the price of winning its Turkish sector. When Damascus fell, the Eastern war—probably the whole war—drew to an end.

Then I was moved by curiosity. "Super flumina Babylonis", read as a boy, had left me longing to feel myself the node of a national movement . . .

There remained historical ambition, insubstantial as a motive by itself. I had dreamed, at the City School in Oxford, of hustling into form, while I lived, the new Asia which time was inexorably bringing upon us. Mecca was to lead to Damascus: Damascus to Anatolia, and afterwards to Bagdad; and then there was Yemen. Fantasies, these will seem, to such as are able to call my beginning an ordinary effort.

Lawrence had the same idealistic and messianic fervour about Arabia as Wilfred Blunt, who after his first visit in 1878 recorded that Arabia was "a romance which more and more absorbed me and determined me to do what I could to help them to preserve their precious gift of independence. Arabia seemed to me in the light of a sacred land, where I had found a mission in life I was bound to fulfil." Lawrence writes that "Upon each return from the East . . . I would visit Wilfred Blunt. An Arab mare drew Blunt's visitors deep within a Sussex wood to his quarried house, stone-flagged and hung with Morris tapestries. There in a great chair he sat, prepared for me like a careless work of art in well-worn Arab robes, his chiselled face framed in silvered, curling hair . . . Blunt was a fire yet flickering over the ashes of old fury . . . How nearly big, as poet, Blunt was. Only his vanity saved him from doing good things in three or four roles". In 1922, the year Blunt died, Lawrence's Arabian career came to an end.

Seven Pillars of Wisdom is Lawrence's narrative of his conduct in the Arab Revolt: "The history is not of the Arab movement, but of me in it." Because Lawrence was more interested in autobiographical than historical truth, he attempts to understand and explain his military, political and emotional experiences. Unlike D'Annunzio and Malraux, who were writers before they were warriors and who use their adventures in war as material for their poetry and fiction, Lawrence's narrative traces the development of his personal relationship with the Arabs, his awareness of the complexity of his feelings and his progress from idealism to disillusionment. Lawrence did not use his experiences to create a hero, but sought to explore, understand and confront his inner self. In *Seven*

Pillars, the effect of war and politics on Lawrence is much more important than the actual historical events.

The Arab Revolt began with a rising in Mecca on June 10, 1916. The Arabs quickly captured Mecca along with Jiddah, the port, and Taif, the summer capital, but they were unable to take Medina, where the large Turkish garrison was quartered. This success in the Eastern theatre of war was especially welcome to the British after the slaughter at Gallipoli in 1915 and the disaster at Kut; but after these initial triumphs and the capture of 6,000 Turkish prisoners, the Revolt became stagnant. At the time of Lawrence's arrival in Jiddah in October 1916, the Arabs had been defeated twice by the Turks. General Glubb states that "the morale of the Arabs was not high, ammunition was scarce, weapons antiquated or unserviceable, and rations precarious. Moreover, the Amir Feisal had no money whatever." The three months that followed the Mecca revolt "were the darkest in the history of the Arab campaign", writes George Antonious. "It looked as though the enemy might possibly recapture Rabegh and march on to Mecca."

Though Lawrence had no previous experience as a military commander, he made a powerful impact on Arabia. He chose Feisal as the Arab leader, provided a liaison between the British and Arab forces, supplied military intelligence, proved his fitness as a leader by enduring hardships and risking his life in the dramatic manner of a Bedouin chieftain, evolved the strategy and tactics for the Revolt, and created the mobile guerrilla army that could conquer the static Turks. The nomadic Arabs lacked the cohesion, collective sense and *esprit de corps* that guerrillas usually possess, and Lawrence states that "it was impossible to mix or combine tribes, since they disliked or distrusted one another." To overcome this weakness, he "combined their loose showers of sparks into a firm flame : transformed their series of unrelated incidents into a conscious operation." As Colonel Stirling writes, "With the help of a few British officers, all senior to himself and professional soldiers, who willingly placed themselves under his general guidance, Lawrence galvanized the Arab Revolt into a coherent whole." And in the history of the Palestine Campaigns, Colonel (later Field Marshal) Wavell summarizes the contribution of Lawrence's Arab army :

Its value to the British commander was great, since it diverted considerable Turkish reinforcements and supplies to the Hejaz, and

protected the right flank of the British armies in their advance through
Palestine. Further, it . . . removed any danger of the establishment
of a German submarine base on the Red Sea. These were important
services, and worth the subsidies in gold and munitions expended
on the Arab forces.

Lawrence's initial strategic decision was to immobilize the 14,000 man
Turkish garrison at Medina and force it into passive defence, instead of
wastefully attacking the heavily fortified town. This plan tied down a
large number of Turkish troops for the duration of the war and forced
the enemy to maintain the thousand-mile Hejaz railway (the target of
endless guerrilla attacks), which had been completed in 1909 to facilitate
the transport of soldiers as well as pilgrims from Damascus to the holy
cities of Arabia.

The first major campaign in which Lawrence implemented his new
strategy, his first and most dramatic victory, and the first moment he
became conscious of his aim in Arabia, was the spectacular capture of
Aqaba in July 1917. This victory involved an extreme example of a
turning movement, a torturous six-hundred mile ride through the desert,
and a descent from the interior on the unguarded eastern side of the
town. The news of the fall of Aqaba coincided with the arrival of the
new commander-in-chief, General Edmund Allenby, whose son had
just been killed in the war. Lawrence adopted Allenby as his second
father-figure; and the General recognized Lawrence's unique military
value, and gave him arms and money as well as complete freedom to
conduct his guerrilla campaigns.

The climactic capture of Aqaba also marked the turning point in
Lawrence's attitude toward the Arabs. At first he admired the Bedouin
and imaginatively identified with them. Their chivalric traditions engaged
his idealistic instincts, their inherent nobility suited his aristocratic background, their group brotherhood answered his loneliness, their silk
embroidered garments satisfied his theatrical narcissism, and their deli-
cious free intimacy appealed to his homosexuality. Lawrence recognized
that male passion had to be satisfied in the desert; and he admired the
"friends quivering together . . . with intimate hot limbs in supreme
embrace." For Lawrence, the clean, indifferent male bodies were not
only a comparatively pure alternative to the raddled meat of prostitutes,
but also had the advantage of providing political as well as sexual unity.

It is clear from Lawrence's description of the moonlit battlefield on the evening of his victory at Aqaba that he felt a perverse fascination with corpses and an intense longing for death.

> The dead men looked wonderfully beautiful. The night was shining gently down, softening them into new ivory. Turks were white-skinned on their clothed parts, much whiter than the Arabs; and these soldiers had been very young. Close round them lapped the dark wormwood, now heavy with dew, in which the ends of the moon-beams sparkled like sea-spray. The corpses seemed flung so pitifully on the ground, huddled anyhow in low heaps. Surely if straightened they would be comfortable at last. So I put them all in order, one by one, very wearied myself, and longing to be of these quiet ones.

Lawrence needed to affirm the sanctity of human life, and to impose a kind of order after the chaos of the Arab plunder through a religious and ritualistic laying out of the corpses. He wanted to relieve his own pain through a sacred and symbolic gesture of merging with the soft decomposing youths; and to ease his guilt and responsibility for what seem to be meaningless deaths.

In the beginning of the war, when the spirit of adventure was still strong, the successful guerrilla raid in which Lawrence shot his own camel during a cavalry charge felt like a schoolboy lark. But after Aqaba the emphasis changed, and his forceful and philosophical speech to his new Arab followers stresses the darker qualities of the Bedouin, suggests the inevitability of Lawrence's tragedy and the radical destruction he must suffer. "There could be no rest-houses for revolt, no dividend of joy paid out. Its spirit was accretive, to endure as far as the senses would endure, and to use each such advance as base for further adventure, deeper privation, sharper pain . . . To the clear-sighted, failure was the only goal. We must believe, through and through, that there was no victory except to go down into death fighting and crying for failure itself." Ultimately, Lawrence was far more attracted to the Arabs' denial of the body that reflected his hatred of the physical, their barrenness and renunciation that suited his asceticism, and their incredible endurance that tested his will and matched his need for self-punishment.

The strain on Lawrence's will began on the Aqaba campaign. As he set out on that agonizing journey "each rest was a blessed relaxation of my will strung to go on"; and at the Howeitat camp he concentrated his powers on "reducing our wills to the single purpose" of endurance and conquest. Lawrence writes that "Akaba had been taken on my plan and by my effort. The cost of it had fallen on my brains and nerves," and that victory led to the disintegration of Lawrence's heroic will and to his progressive mental, moral, spiritual and physical deterioration (he now weighed less than one hundred pounds). Lawrence endured dysentery and delirium, thirst and starvation, boils and bruises, stings and bites, torture and degradation; and as he began to break down under the increasing strain, he made even greater demands upon himself. In his attempt to destroy the Yarmuk bridge, he rode eighty miles in thirteen hours of darkness; and during the railway detonation at Mifleh, he suffered lacerations, a fracture and five bullet wounds, and was confronted with the horror of "the scalded and smoking upper half" of a victim on the train.

Lawrence was driven by the will to power and employed this impulse to create an Arab empire. Lawrence writes in the suppressed introductory chapter of *Seven Pillars,* "I presumed (seeing no other leader with *the will and the power*) that I would survive the campaigns, and be able to defeat not merely the Turks on the battlefield, but my own country and its allies in the council-chamber." And this, almost precisely, is what Lawrence did, by will, from almost nothing.

The supremacy of the will is affirmed by the force of its opposition. As Nietzsche states:

It is *not* the satisfaction of the will that causes pleasure . . . but rather the will's forward thrust and again and again becoming master over that which stands in its way. The feeling of pleasure lies precisely in the dissatisfaction of the will, in the fact that the will is never satisfied unless it has opponents and resistance.

This perception cuts to the core of Lawrence's psychology, for he had a masochistic, almost Sisyphean pleasure in the resistance, the subjection and even the destruction of his will.

In an insightful letter, Aldous Huxley describes the paradox of Lawrence's heroic will and wounded spirit:

He had everything that the human individual, as an individual, can possess—talent, courage, indomitable will, intelligence, everything, and his gifts permitted him to do extraordinary, hardly credible things . . . Lawrence had a self-will of heroic, even Titanic proportions; and one has the impression that he lived for the most part in one of the more painful corners of the inferno.

But Lawrence could never have reached the height of his creative genius without suffering infernal torments. It is almost as if, in these agonizing moments, he became pure mind, disembodied from his corporal substance. In Arabia, Lawrence, the "tragic-warlike man," was annealed into knowledge, and achieved his most acute intellectual and psychological perceptions when he suffered pain most acutely : when racked by disease and tortured by the Turkish Bey.

The strain of fever and exhaustion brought Lawrence to the breaking point at Abu Markha. "About ten days I lay in that tent, suffering a bodily weakness which made my animal self crawl away and hide till the shame was passed. As usual in such circumstances my mind cleared, my senses became more acute, and I began to think consecutively of the Arab Revolt, as an accustomed duty to rest upon against the pain." The result of this reflection was his brilliant theory of guerrilla warfare. For Lawrence, endurance and pain led to self-knowledge, and the Nietzschean will to power transformed this knowledge into action and thrust him on his spiritual quest that led to Damascus.

Despite the strain, Lawrence's will endured until his terrible torture at Deraa in November 1917, the most important and influential moment in his life. In chapter 80 of *Seven Pillars* Lawrence relates that he went on a secret reconnaissance behind enemy lines disguised as a Circassian, was arrested by a Turkish sergeant, and brought before the Bey who offered to pay Lawrence if he would love him. When Lawrence refused, the Turkish soldier tore his clothes away, bit by bit, until he resisted and jerked his knee into the Bey's groin.

The soldiers seized Lawrence and the Bey "spat at me swearing he would make me ask pardon." He beat Lawrence with a bedroom slipper, "leaned forward, fixed his teeth in my neck and bit till the blood came." Afterward the Bey drew a bayonet, and in a movement of symbolic virgin-violation "pulled up a fold of the flesh over my ribs, worked the point through, after considerable trouble, and gave the blade a half-turn. This hurt, and I winced, while the blood wavered down my side . . . He looked pleased." Lawrence then reveals :

In my despair I spoke. His face changed and he stood still, then controlled his voice with an effort to say significantly, "You must understand that I know : and it will be easier if you do as I wish." I was dumbfounded, and we stared silently at one another, while the men who felt an inner meaning beyond their experience, shifted uncomfortably. But it was evidently a chance shot, by which he himself did not, or would not, mean what I feared.

The more likely meanings of "You must understand that I know" are that after the angry Lawrence told the Turk he was sexually depraved, the Turk, who had Lawrence exposed, degraded and literally at his mercy, realized that Lawrence was not what he pretended to be (an ordinary Circassian) and recognized that Lawrence (like himself) was a sado-masochist and a homosexual.

Lawrence was next taken out and beaten, and his moment of self-insight came when his will was completely shattered by the unbearable brutality.

> He began to lash me madly across and across with all his might, while I locked my teeth to endure this thing which lapped itself like flaming wire about my body. . . . I could feel only the shapeless weight of pain, not tearing claws, for which I had been prepared, but a gradual cracking apart of my whole being by some too-great force whose waves rolled up my spine till they were pent within my brain, to clash terribly together. . . . [The men] would squabble for the next turn, ease themselves, and play unspeakably with me. . . . A hard white ridge, like a railway darkening slowly into crimson, leaped over my skin at the instant of each stroke, with a bead of blood where two ridges crossed. As the punishment proceeded the whip fell more and more upon existing weals, biting blacker or more wet, till my flesh quivered with accumulated pain, and with terror of the next blow coming. . . . At last I was completely broken.

The sadistic ingenuity of the depraved torturers was as fearful as humiliation, suffering or death; and this extreme moment represented the ultimate punishment for Lawrence's accumulated fear and guilt. As in Kafka's Penal Colony, the crime was literally imprinted on the body of the victim. The "flaming wire" and "railway darkening into crimson" reflect not only Lawrence's unsuccessful railroad detonations but also his guilt about the bloody deaths of innocent civilians who had been killed by his successful explosions. The homosexual rape ("ease themselves") led to the terrifying realization that a part of him wanted to be sodomized, and in the midst of this torture the sado-masochism and homosexuality of the illegitimate, celibate and ascetic Lawrence are suddenly revealed:

> I remembered the corporal kicking me with his nailed boot . . . and remembered smiling idly at him, for a delicious warmth, probably sexual, was swelling through me.

In this terrifying epiphany Lawrence overcame his obsessive childhood fear of pain and became like the Arabs, for whom pain was "a solvent, a cathartic, almost a decoration, to be fairly worn while they survived it." But the punishment for this perverse pleasure was instantaneous:

> He flung up his arms and hacked with the full length of his whip into my groin. This doubled me half-over, screaming, or rather, trying impotently to scream, only shuddering through my open mouth. . . . Another slash followed. A roaring, and my eyes went black: while within me the core of life seemed to heave slowly up through the rending nerves, expelled from its body by this last indescribable pang.

We have seen that during the preliminary perversions Lawrence had kicked the Bey in the testicles, and it seems clear from this passage that "the core of life" that heaves up slowly like an orgasm is Lawrence's oblique metaphorical revelation that the unbearable pain in his sexual organs forced him to give in to the rape and that he was rendered physically as well as spiritually impotent by the vengeful Bey.

The longer, unpublished Oxford version (1922) of the torture concludes with a long, sensitive, poignant passage, omitted from the published text, in which Lawrence probes deeper into his seared psyche than anywhere else and reveals that longing for self-immolation that would not leave him for the rest of his life.

> I was feeling very ill, as though some part of me had gone dead that night in Deraa, leaving me maimed, imperfect, only half myself. It could not have been the defilement, for no one ever held the body in less honour than I did myself. Probably it had been the breaking of the spirit by that frenzied nerve-shattering pain which had degraded me to the beast level when it made me grovel to it, and which had journeyed with me since, a fascination and terror and morbid desire, lascivious and vicious, perhaps, but like the striving of a moth towards its flame.

In another letter to Charlotte Shaw, written in 1928, Lawrence revives the earlier themes of his mother's dominance, his frightening similarity to her, his ambivalent attraction-repulsion, her probing search into his privacy, her vicarious existence in her children's lives, and her insatiable demand for love, especially after the death of two of her sons in the war, and clarifies the meaning of the torture at Deraa.

> She is monumental really : and so unlike you. Probably she is exactly like me; otherwise we wouldn't so hanker after one another, whenever we are wise enough to keep apart. Her letters are things I dread, and she always asks for more of mine (I try to write monthly : but we haven't a subject we dare to be intimate upon : so they are spavined things) and hates them when they come, as they do, ever so rarely. I think I'm afraid of letting her get, ever so little, inside the circle of my integrity : and she is always hammering and sapping to come in. A very dominant person : only old now, and, so my brother says, very much less than she had been. She has lived so in her children, & in my father, that she cannot relieve herself, upon herself, and from herself, at all. And it isn't right to cry out to your children for love. They are presented by the walls of time and function, from loving their parents.

Lawrence's language in this letter is strikingly close to his description of his torture and rape at Deraa. His mother's "sapping" is a metaphor of siege and assault, and also has the suggestion of sexual debilitation. Lawrence's terror that if she knew his feelings "they would be damaged : *violated* : no longer mine" (in the earlier letter to Charlotte Shaw) and his fear "of letting her get . . . inside the circle of my *integrity*" is emotionally and psychologically connected to the last sentence of the Deraa chapter : "the passing days confirmed how in Deraa that night the citadel of my integrity had been irrevocably lost." The greatest childhood fear of his mother was realized in the most horrible and degrading moment of Lawrence's life.

The Deraa experience taught Lawrence, who tried to make himself pure will, that the spirit is ultimately dependent on the body, and it led him into nihilism. "The practice of our revolt fortified the nihilist attitude in me. During it, we often saw men push themselves or be driven to a cruel extreme of endurance : yet never was there an intimation of physical break. Collapse rose always from a moral weakness eating into the body, which of itself, without traitors from within, had no power over the will." When Lawrence discovered that he had a perverse sexual nature, the "traitor within", his will broke and he collapsed.

The torture at Deraa completely destroyed Lawrence's elaborately constructed network of defences and exposed his pathetic yet all-too-human vulnerability. This assault by the despised Turkish enemy on the point of his greatest weakness, his sexual core, subverted his powers of endurance, betrayed the high ideals of the dedicatory poem to Dahoum, and ravished his bodily integrity. Lawrence could never forgive himself for succumbing to bodily pain, for as Erik Erikson writes of the creative man : "he must court sickness, failure, or insanity, in order to test the alternative whether the established world will crush him, or whether he will disestablish a sector of this world's outworn fundaments and make a place for a new one." The Deraa torture dramatized a central conflict in Lawrence's life : for when the will was crushed, the possibilities of creative freedom seemed extinguished.

After the capture of Aqaba, and especially after Deraa, Lawrence's mood became extremely pessimistic. Broken by the strain of his ordeal in Arabia, he could no longer reconcile his opposing selves : the one who had conquered by a ruthless exercise of power, the other who knew that these victories led to personal degradation. Lawrence moved from brotherhood to isolation, from heroism to revulsion, from idealism to nihilism. He felt guilty about the bloodshed and the deaths; his scrupulous conscience was disturbed by his ultimate failure to identify with the Arabs and by his inability to realize his ideals; and he was tormented by the need to betray the Arabs to English political interests.

Not for the first or last time service to two masters irked me. I was one of Allenby's officers, and in his confidence : in return, he expected me to do the best I could for him. I was Feisal's adviser, and Feisal relied upon the honesty and competence of my advice so far as often to take it without argument. Yet I could not explain to Allenby the whole Arab situation, nor disclose the full British plan to Feisal.

Lawrence's idealism and honour, and his ambiguous role as English commander, liaison and adviser in the Arab Revolt, made him extremely vulnerable to political conflicts; and his need to compromise his principles and take up his "mantle of fraud in the East" for military reasons made him very bitter.

The great victories that Lawrence achieved in the last half of the war

as the Arabs fought northwards to Damascus, though significant from
the military viewpoint, merely intensified his deep despair. The entry
into Jerusalem after seven hunded years of Moslem rule; the classic
battle of Seil El-Hasa in which he surprised and destroyed the Turkish
right flank and then charged through their centre line, killing the
commander, slaughtering the troops, capturing all the artillery and taking
250 prisoners; and even the total rout of the Turkish Fourth Army, led
to a military triumph and an emotional collapse.

The long-awaited capture of Damascus was not a joyous fulfilment
of the Arabs' goal, and the anarchic chaos of the city, "half insane with
religious enthusiasm," revealed that the tribal Arabs lacked a national
identity and could not unite and rule themselves effectively. "Such
carnival as the town had not held for six hundred years" was celebrated
in the "streets paved with corpses, the gutters running blood."

The conquest of Damascus was also contaminated by the sickening
stench of the Turkish hospital, an embodiment of Goya's *Disasters of
War*, where the rats gnawed wet red galleries into the putrescent
corpses. This was the climax of the entire campaign and the culmination
of all the slaughter : from the unwilling execution of his wounded friend
Farraj, who blessed Lawrence and at last wearily closed his eyes to make
the terrible deed easier, to the "faceless man, spraying blood from a
fringe of red flesh about his neck." "This killing and killing of Turks
is horrible," Lawrence wrote in 1917. "You charge in at the finish and
find them all over the place in bits, and still alive many of them, and
know that you have done hundreds in the same way before and must
do hundreds more if you can." In the phantasmagoric hospital, Lawrence
seemed faced with the corpse of every man he had ever killed—nause-
ously chromatic, putrid, swollen, burst open and liquescent with decay.
The mass burial in the common grave has the elaborately detailed description that Lawrence reserved for the most revolting and morbid moments
of his life : "The trench was small for them, but so fluid was the mass
that each newcomer, when tipped in, fell softly, just jellying out the
edges of the pile a little with his weight." Lawrence was obsessed by
physical pain, disfigurement and death; and in *Seven Pillars* he was
able to transmute horror into shocking but beautiful images—bloody
snow like watermelon or corpses like new ivory—and to suggest the
beauty that, for him, was inherent in pain. He kept photographs of
the Turkish wounded in his home at Clouds Hill (an elaborate reproduc-

tion of his boyhood garden cottage) and often studied their gruesome details.

The Arab nationalists in Damascus were encouraged by D'Annunzio's defiance of the Paris Peace Conference and his successful capture of Fiume, for both D'Annunzio and Lawrence opposed the Allies' secret treaties, crowned their military careers with the capture of Fiume and Damascus, and challenged the Great Powers in Paris. Both men were charismatic commanders who worshipped speed and machinery, led their men into action and inspired their passionate devotion, conducted their private campaigns outside the regular chain of command, projected their sexual attitudes into their military adventures, were wounded and decorated for heroism, and helped to create their own legends. Though the followers of D'Annunzio and of Lawrence were both driven out of their captured cities, the Italians were triumphantly vindicated when Mussolini "settled" the Fiume question just as the Arabs were when Lawrence "settled" the Middle East. Both D'Annunzio and Lawrence were exhausted by their military service and postwar politics, and were removed from power at the same time. Both withdrew from the world and spent the long, last phase of their lives in seclusion : D'Annunzio in sybaritic splendour at the Vittoriale, Lawrence in ascetic renunciation in the barracks. While D'Annunzio wrote poetry and collected cruisers and torpedo-boats, Lawrence translated what he liked to call "Chapman's Homer" on the Northwest Frontier of India (1927-1928) and developed high-speed rescue boats (1929-1935).

Lawrence's postwar life—his diplomatic and political careers, the composition of *Seven Pillars,* the enlistment in the ranks, the ritualistic scourgings and even the suicidal motorcycle rides—followed inevitably from his experience in the war. For just as every aspect of his early life prepared for and led up to his campaign in Arabia, so everything that happened after it was a direct result of those two years that synthesized the experience of a lifetime.

Lawrence correctly believed that the British Cabinet "raised the Arabs to fight for us by definite promises of self-government afterwards." But in order to gain military and political support during the war, the British government made two other contradictory pledges : to the French in the Sykes-Picot Treaty of 1916, and to the Jews in the Balfour Declaration of 1917. Nevertheless, Lawrence was determined to redeem his personal honour by fulfilling the British pledges to the Arabs; and he explained his divided loyalties in the bitterly angry original introduction to *Seven Pillars.*

In this chapter, which was suppressed on the advice of Bernard Shaw and first published in 1939, Lawrence emphasizes the importance of the Arab victory and writes, with some oversimplification and distortion, that his book "is just a designed procession of Arab freedom from Mecca to Damascus . . . It was an Arab war waged and led by Arabs for an Arab aim in Arabia." He then descends from this high idealism to an intense disillusionment with imperialistic greed.

> We were casting them by thousands into the fire to the worst of deaths, not to win the war but that the corn and rice and oil of Mesopotamia might be ours. . . . But when we won, it was charged against me that the British petrol royalties in Mesopotamia were become dubious, and French colonial policy ruined in the Levant. I am afraid that I hope so. We pay for these things too much in honour and in innocent lives.

In *Seven Pillars* Lawrence laments, "Clearly I had no shadow of leave to engage the Arabs, unknowing, in a gamble of life and death. Inevitably and justly we should reap bitterness, a sorry fruit of heroic endeavour." And in the suppressed chapter, he describes his anguished feelings and his hope for a just fulfilment of British pledges to the Arabs.

> I had to join the conspiracy, and . . . I was continually and bitterly ashamed. It was evident from the beginning that if we won the war these promises would be dead paper, and had I been an honest adviser of the Arabs I would have advised them to go home and not risk their lives fighting for such stuff : but I salved myself with the hope that, by leading these Arabs madly in the final victory I would establish them, with arms in their hands, in a position so assured (if not dominant) that expediency would counsel to the Great Powers a fair settlement of their claims.

On February 6, 1919 Feisal, representing his father Sherif Hussein, and Lawrence, serving as Feisal's adviser and interpreter (he addressed the diplomats in English, French and Arabic), presented their case at the Paris Peace Conference. Liddell Hart writes that "the voice of Lawrence, who had constituted himself counsel for the Arab cause, carried penetratingly through the ante-chambers of Versailles, into the innermost chambers. . . . On Lloyd George especially his arguments made an impression, helped by the British Prime Minister's instinctive sympathy towards the rights of small or submerged peoples." At one point when the French Foreign Minister was discoursing on France's historic claim to Syria, based on the Crusades, Feisal quietly destroyed his argument by asking: "But which of us *won* the Crusades?"

Because Feisal's claims for the Arabs opposed French interests in Syria, France insisted that Britain adhere to the secret Sykes-Picot Treaty, which divided the Middle East between France and England. In September 1919 the British yielded to French pressure and agreed to a military evacuation of Syria, and the troops that had for a year supported Feisal's government against French intervention left on November 1st.

In March 1920, the Arab Congress in Damascus proclaimed Feisal King of Syria; and at the San Remo Conference in April 1920, France was given the mandate for Syria and Britain the mandate for Palestine and Mesopotamia. Feisal attempted to moderate the Arab extremists, but there was naturally some armed resistance to the French occupation, and he was given an ultimatum on July 14th. Though Feisal agreed to most of the terms, the French army under General Gouraud advanced on Damascus, occupied the city on July 25th, and drove him out of Syria. Feisal's expulsion marked the lowest point of Lawrence's and the Arabs' political fortunes; and Churchill writes: "I am sure that the ordeal of watching the helplessness of his Arab friends to whom he had pledged his word, and, as he conceived it, the word of Britain, maltreated in this horrible manner, must have been the main cause of his eventual renunciation of all power in great affairs." It was characteristic of the idealistic Lawrence to bind his personal honour to the political promises of his country.

In February 1921, when Lawrence was appointed political adviser to Churchill, the Secretary of State for Dominions and Colonies, he was finally able to use his powerful influence to achieve a satisfactory political solution in the Middle East. Lawrence provided the technical advice and persuasive arguments for Churchill's decisions at the Cairo Conference of March 1921, which placed Feisal on the throne of Iraq (Mesopotamia) and his brother Abdullah on that of Transjordan. St. John Philby, who opposed Lawrence in Cairo and advocated the leadership of King Saud, states that Lawrence "succeeded in making everyone who mattered believe that his solution was the right one. Lloyd George, Curzon, Churchill, Clemenceau, Hogarth and others were not people to be easily deceived: and they all, in one way or another, gave him their support in his scheme for placing the destinies of the Arab world at the mercy of the Hashemite dynasty." And Churchill says of Lawrence's visit to Amman in September 1921 to sort out the postwar chaos in Transjordan: "He had plenary powers. He wielded them with his old vigour. He removed officers. He used force. He restored complete tranquillity."

Lawrence believed that his political accomplishments in 1921, when Churchill fulfilled "our promises in letter and spirit (where humanly possible) without sacrificing any interest of our empire or any interest of the peoples concerned," was a harder and better effort than his military victory. And in a "Draft Preface" to *Seven Pillars* in 1922, Lawrence evaluates his political achievement and ends in a resigned and rather bitter tone.

> I do not wish to publish secret documents, nor to make long explanations: but must put on record my conviction that England is out of the Arab affair with clean hands. . . . I showed the Arabs my wounds (over sixty I have, and each scar evidence of a pain incurred in Arab service), as proof I had worked sincerely on their side. They found me out-of-date: and I was happy to withdraw from a political milieu which had never been congenial.

Lawrence's background and training made him superbly suited to record a movement and a country and a race in the last of the picturesque wars; and at the Peace Conference in February 1919, he began the composition of his masterpiece. Lawrence admits that the book "might have been happier, had I foreseen the clean ending [of the Arab settlement]. I wrote it in some stress and misery of mind." In view of Lawrence's condition at the end of the war, it is extraordinary that he could begin to write at all.

Two of Lawrence's brothers had been killed in France in 1915, his young friend Dahoum died in 1918, and his father succumbed in the influenza epidemic of April 1919. The following month Lawrence, who was wounded nine times in the war and had suffered brutal torture, crashed in Rome while flying to Cairo to collect his papers. The two pilots in the front seat of the small plane were killed when they attempted a night landing, overshot the airport and flew into a quarry. Lawrence suffered a concussion, a broken collar-bone and ribs, and a damaged lung that troubled him for the rest of his life.

The war made Lawrence an "extinct volcano", and like Conrad's Lord Jim and Razumov, he experienced a moral self-betrayal and dishonorable fall from self-esteem that intensified his masochistic guilt. In 1919, less than a year after the capture of Damascus, as Lawrence was writing *Seven Pillars* and his fears about the English betrayal of the Arabs were being realized at the Peace Conference, Lowell Thomas began his illustrated lectures on Lawrence's career at Covent Garden. Lawrence, like Byron, awoke one morning to find himself famous. Thomas' lectures (which Lawrence secretly attended) transformed the horrible reality of the war into a glamorous myth and placed him in a painful position. Though Lawrence's fame as a Prince of the Desert was pleasurable for a time, the contrast between the public and private image of himself, an important theme in *Seven Pillars,* only exacerbated his guilt.

After the disappointments of the Peace Conference Lawrence was awarded a Fellowship at All Souls for 1919–1920, and he continued to write in the attic of Sir Herbert Baker's house at 14 Barton Street in Westminster. Lawrence first wrote a synopsis and then the individual chapters of *Seven Pillars* with a compulsive frenzy, and he confesses to friends that the book "went through four versions in the four years I struggled with it, and I gave it all my nights and days till I was nearly blind and mad. . . . I excited myself with hunger and cold and sleeplessness more than did de Quincey with his opium." Lawrence claimed that the book was written in sittings of 22–24 hours, averaging 1000–1500 words an hour, and that the whole of Book 6 was completed between sunrise and sunrise. In order to recreate his experiences, to transmute his suffering into art and to exorcise the demons of guilt in a sacrificial offering to the spirit of the Arabs, Lawrence made the writing of the book almost as painful as the war itself. He could still feel the wounds of Arabia and the scars of Deraa stood out on his back.

The example of Charles Doughty gave Lawrence a human model, a personal inspiration and a literary example of a modern man who had submerged himself in the life and language of Arabia. Since Lawrence spent many years among the same nomadic Bedouin of the Nejd and the Hejaz, endured the same weariness of forced marches, and the same loneliness and misery in the struggle against the torments of the desert, it was inevitable that Lawrence's book, like his life, would be influenced by a work with which he had such strong affinities. The powerful sense in *Seven Pillars* of a search for spiritual self-redemption evolves not only from Lawrence's study of the Crusaders and his interest in medieval romance from Malory to Morris, but also from the inspiration of Doughty's Mosaic wanderings and fierce ordeals.

For both Doughty and Lawrence the essential characteristic of Arabia is its elemental rage, and both men insist on measuring themselves against the pitiless Arab standard of endurance. At the end of the battles that have nearly destroyed him Lawrence confesses: "my body so dreaded further pain that now I had to force myself under fire. Generally, I had been hungry, lately always cold: and frost and dirt had poisoned my hurts into a festering mass of sores." Throughout *Seven Pillars* the desert landscapes reflect Lawrence's seared soul; and when he was forced to execute the Bedouin murderer to avoid a tribal blood feud, the weight of the climate and the shape of the land, the constructive and deathly gulley, became an active and threatening force. Both Doughty and Lawrence paid dearly for their books and created literature out of suffering.

Seven Pillars exhibits Lawrence's conflicting desires for self-revelation and for obscurity, and the fastidious private edition of 1926 was a compromise that allowed him to communicate obliquely his terrible truths to a carefully selected audience without exposing himself to the general public. The immense care he took with the minute aesthetic details of the book suggest his compulsive fascination with his experiences and his desire to extend the torments of the war for seven more years. Writing about the Arabian campaign gave Lawrence the opportunity to reveal and resolve the conflicts in loyalty he had suffered and to discharge his obligation to the Arabs. His guilt about their political betrayal was combined with his anguish about the torture at Deraa, so that the writing of the book answered his moral as well as his psychological needs. *Seven Pillars* is the story of Lawrence's growth in personal and political awareness. Its meaning is determined by his motivations and character as well as by the pattern of historical events, by the conflict between the man who acts and the conditions of his action. The book is at once a story of a search for self-knowledge and a narrative of physical effort, a spiritual autobiography and a confession of destruction and renunciation.

In August 1922, when his political work in the Middle East was completed and a satisfactory version of *Seven Pillars* finished, Lawrence rejected Churchill's offer to succeed General Allenby as High Commissioner in Egypt, abandoned the unlimited possibilities of a career in public life, voluntarily returned to his mother's class, and (using the name John Hume Ross) enlisted in the masculine ranks of the R.A.F. Not since Rimbaud abandoned poetry had there been such a dramatic renunciation; and Lawrence's motives for plunging into the squalor of an air force depot are extremely complex.

Lawrence had rejected the possibility of a professional career. He could not practise archaeology in the Middle East without political surveillance, and he was not interested in exploring other civilizations. He refused to benefit in any way from his achievements in Arabia, declined military honours and important positions, and would not accept money for journalism or for *Seven Pillars*. As David Hogarth explained to Bernard Shaw: "Lawrence is not normal in many ways and it is extraordinarily difficult to do anything for him. . . . He will not work in any sort of harness unless this is padlocked onto him. He enlisted in order to have the padlocks riveted onto him."

After the war, when Lawrence's will could no longer drive his body and his asceticism degenerated into a tragic wish for annihilation, he felt the need for riveted padlocks.

I was tired to death of free-will, and of many things besides free-will. For a year and a half I had been in motion, riding a thousand miles each month upon camels: with added nervous hours in crazy aeroplanes, or rushing across country in powerful cars. In the last five actions I had been hit. . . . These worries would have taken their due petty place, in my despite of the body, and of my soiled body in particular, but for the rankling fraudulence which had to be my mind's habit. . . . My will had gone and I feared to be alone, lest the winds of circumstance, or power, or lust, blow my empty soul away.

Lawrence's death wish, which could be displaced but not eliminated, combined with the intense strain of the Paris and Cairo Conferences and the exhausting composition of *Seven Pillars,* led to a severe physical and mental breakdown immediately before his enlistment.

Jock Chambers, a close friend of Lawrence during his years in the R.A.F., has told me that Lawrence was completely shattered when he joined up, and he writes that "When asleep he continually repeated a horrible experience of his war-time days." Another friend reports that after Lawrence enlisted, "He had got into such a state of nerves that he found himself locking himself up in lavatories and sobbing endlessly, time after time." As Lawrence wrote in 1922 : "I'm afraid (physically afraid) of other men : their animal spirits seem to me the most terrible companions to haunt a man. . . . What is it that makes me so damnably sensitive and so ready to cry out, and yet so ready to incur more pain?" Because of his torture at Deraa Lawrence, who had developed a morbid, neurotic negation of life, wanted to hide, to escape respectability, to test his weakened will and his infinite capacity for suffering. *The Mint* (1928), Lawrence's brutal account of his first six months in the R.A.F., reveals that his quest for psychological martyrdom in the Arabian campaign ("The virtue of sacrifice lay within the victim's soul"), became a reality in the air force.

The penultimate paragraph of the Epilogue to *Seven Pillars* suggests yet another convincing reason for his retreat into obscurity. Lawrence writes : "We took Damascus, and I feared. More than three arbitrary days would have quickened in me a root of authority" ("*vice* of authority" in the Oxford edition). Lawrence's great gift was his extraordinary power to influence and command everyone he ever met, and no one has been able to analyse or explain this mysterious power. Even the soul-searching Lawrence did not completely understand it, though he was clearly fascinated by the connection between authority, power and destruction. Colonel Richard Meinertzhagen, who knew Lawrence well, states that he "was a man who held physical power in awe, he almost worshipped it. He once said to me. 'It must be a delightful sensation to be so strong that one can do as one likes with anyone.' " In a revealing letter to Charlotte Shaw, Lawrence says that power, especially the power to kill, terrified him and forced him to relinquish all authority and to submerge himself in a humble position : "So long as there is breath in my body my strength will be exerted to keep my soul in prison, since nowhere else can it exist in safety. The terror of being run away with, in the liberty of power, lies at the back of these many renunciations of my later life. I am afraid, of myself. Is this madness?"

When Lawrence's identity was discovered in January 1923 he was discharged from the R.A.F. and forced to spend two dreadful years in the Tank Corps before he was readmitted (under the name of T. E. Shaw) to the air force in August 1925. Lawrence's final and most profound analysis of the question of will occurs in the extraordinary letters he wrote to Lionel Curtis from the animal lair of the Tank Corps barracks in 1923. "The burning out of free-will and self-respect and delicacy from a nature as violent as mine is bound to hurt a bit. . . . Free-will I've tried, and rejected. . . . action I've rejected : and the intellectual life : and the receptive senses : and the battle of wits. They were all failures." In this letter Lawrence turns away finally from the first two phases of his life and character : as a man of knowledge and a man of action. He had paid dearly for his triumphs and was transfigured into suffering.

Lawrence's isolation and agony forced his eccentric genius into nihilism, and his retreat in to the ranks was a substitute for madness or suicide. As he confessed to Lionel Curtis, "This sort of thing must be madness, and sometimes I wonder how far mad I am, and if a madhouse would not be my next (and merciful) stage. Merciful compared with this place, which hurts me, body and soul." When, writes Lawrence, the will can no longer lead to the oblivion of activity, "there seemed a certainty in degradation, a final safety. . . . Sometimes we wish for chains as a variety." In Zarathustra's words, "To those who are as restless as you, even a jail will at last seem bliss. Have you ever seen how imprisoned criminals sleep? They sleep calmly, enjoying their new security."

Lawrence's sexual surrender at Deraa and his homosexuality that was so inextricably a part of it, led not only to a retreat into the ranks but also to an intense desire for self-punishment and humiliation. Lawrence told Lionel Curtis that his masochism remains and will remain, and emphasizes that self-degradation was his aim. "I long for people to look down on me and despise me," he writes to Charlotte Shaw, "and I'm too shy to take the filthy steps which would publicly shame me, and put me in their contempt".

Even life in the ranks could not satisfy Lawrence's self-hatred, and he constantly attempted to punish himself through starvation, asceticism, masochism and even flagellation : "Everything bodily is now hateful to me". To prove that his will could dominate his body he often resorted to trials of physical endurance that made his mind an objective observer of his suffering flesh and threw his spirit into greater relief. St. John Philby reports that on a freezing ride through Jordan in 1921, "we travelled ourselves on the engine, cowering as near the boiler as possible against the icy wind and driving sleet. Lawrence stood out on the dashboard during the whole journey of three or four hours." And while serving in the Tank Corps in 1923, Lawrence persuaded a young Scotsman, John Bruce, to flog him at regular intervals, sometimes on the anniversary of the Deraa torture, over the extended period of eleven years. This ritualistic flagellation revived the sexual pleasure as well as the sexual guilt of Deraa, but did not bring the redemption that the medieval flagellants hoped to achieve.

Though the precise reasons for Lawrence's scourging are obscure, it is likely that the series of beatings exemplify the "repetition-compulsion" that Freud discusses in *Beyond the Pleasure Principle* and relates to the death-instinct The whippings were a re-enactment of Lawrence's terrible traumatic guilt, and allowed him to redeem his eternal and existential debt by enduring what had once crushed his body and spirit, and to displace the death-instinct with self-punishment instead of self-destruction. Lawrence's death wish was embodied in the frenetic speed passage in "The Road" section of the masochistic *Mint* and finally realized a few months after his release from the R.A.F. in the fatal yet predestined motorcycle accident of May 1935.

Malraux's description of Lawrence's dominant characteristics suggests that this Faustian seeker to the extremes of madness was torn from within by the antithesis between body and will, nihilism and idealism, the real world and the world he wished to create. Lawrence had a

> taste for self-humiliation, now by discipline, now by veneration; a horror of respectability; a disgust for possessions . . . a thoroughgoing sense of guilt, pursued by his angels or his minor demons, a sense of evil, and of the nothingness of almost everything men cling to; a need for the absolute, an instinctive taste for asceticism.

Lawrence's role in the Arab Revolt combined self-discipline with immense freedom and power, and his devotion to the higher cause of a "holy war" enabled him to define his identity and to discover the sensitive and artistic inner core that was surrounded by an envelope of aggression and action. But for Lawrence this self-discovery was destructive rather than enlightening, for when he was beaten and raped at Deraa he realized that he was a homosexual and that he could get physical pleasure from pain.

Lawrence's campaign in Arabia revealed how a scholarly and high-minded young man could be destroyed, not only by suffering cruelty in war, but also by his unlimited power to wound and to kill. He gradually realized that he had entered the war as a man who valued human life and gave himself in the service of freedom, and that he had been transformed into a man who was caught up in the repellent and fascinating slaughter and had lost his idealism and even his desire to live.

ANDRÉ MALRAUX

(b. 1901)

I lie, but my lies become truths.

MALRAUX

André Malraux has always admired intellectual men of action : Trotsky, Mao, De Gaulle, and he believes "A man is what he does." The pattern and meaning of Malraux's complex life becomes clearer when he is compared to Gabriele D'Annunzio, T. E. Lawrence and Marie-David de Mayrena, who belonged to a vanished breed of mythomanic adventurers, who believed their own lies and turned them into legends, and who were able to live out their private fantasies. D'Annunzio and Lawrence, who reached the peak of their careers just as Malraux began his own brilliant trajectory through art, war and politics, were the most immediate and influential models of the literary adventurer.

In the 1920s Malraux wanted to be, like D'Annunzio, a stylish revolutionary *condottiere* who could inspire and lead a people to nationalistic glory. His first wife, Clara, reports in her perceptive but bitchy memoirs that after Malraux's arrest in Indochina he boasted, " 'Don't lose heart : I'll certainly end up by being Gabriele D'Annunzio.' Where did I find the strength to shout that I did not care a damn in hell for Gabriele D'Annunzio, that grotesque, indecent clown? The funny thing is," writes Clara forty years after the incident, "that he has really become Gabriele D'Annunzio."

Throughout his life Malraux has been obsessed by T. E. Lawrence, whom he sees as the archetypal scholar, soldier and writer, as well as the Nietzschean precursor of Malraux's own fight against destiny and attempt at self-transcendence. Both Lawrence and Malraux deliberately disguised their family background and the major events of their lives, and created their own exotic legends as an attractive alternative to reality. As Malraux writes of the Lawrencean hero of *The Walnut Trees of Altenburg* (1943): "He could perhaps have found some means of destroying the mythical person he was growing into, had he been compelled. But he had no wish to do so. His reputation was flattering. What was more important, he enjoyed it."

Both Lawrence and Malraux possessed a formidable erudition in their youth, despised academic pedantry, were fascinated by remote civilizations and cultures, began their careers with archaeological expeditions to the East and carried out explorations in the desert. Both flamboyantly led the underdog in a foreign war and became fascinated with flying. Both were war heroes who shifted from a military to a political career at a crucial moment in history, and became the intellectual and ideological supporters of nationalistic leaders: Feisal and De Gaulle. While Lawrence deliberately regressed from a Lieutenant-Colonel to a private in the Tank Corps, Malraux, who adopted Lawrence's guerrilla tactics when he fought with the Resistance, began as a private in the Tank Corps and became a Lieutenant-Colonel. Malraux's capture of Strasbourg, the last French city in German hands, at the head of the Alsace-Lorraine Brigade, was the symbolic equivalent of Lawrence's capture of Damascus, the last Arab city in Turkish hands, at the head of the Bedouin legions. In *The Walnut Trees of Altenburg* Malraux observes, "Intellectuals are like women . . . soldiers make them dream," and in his own life he attempted to turn his dream of Lawrence into reality.

Malraux planned to write the life of Lawrence as early as 1929 and a chapter from this book, "Lawrence and the Demon of the Absolute" (1946), was written in 1942 at the same time as *The Walnut Trees of Altenburg,* in which Vincent Berger's tribal warfare among the Senussi of the Libyan desert and his relation to Enver Pasha and the Pan-Turk movement are clearly based on Lawrence's achievements in the Arab Revolt. In his essay on Lawrence, Malraux remarks, "Whoever writes his memoirs (except to deceive) judges himself. There were in this book [*Seven Pillars of Wisdom*], as in all memoirs, two *personae*: the one who said I and the author." This statement is revealing because Malraux's *Antimemoirs* (1967) were influenced by Lawrence's confessional mode and by his two *personae,* and also because Malraux's analysis and judgment of Lawrence represent a synthesis of his own dominant characteristics:

His pride; his appetite for glory and deceit, his scorn of this desire; his implacable will; his distrust of ideas; his need for relief from his intelligence; his anguished self-consciousness which led him to try to see himself through the eyes of others; his lack of all faith and the search for the limits of his strength.

Finally, just as Malraux, when a student in 1914, is said to have met D'Annunzio in Paris, so in an interview with *L'Express* in 1971 Malraux claimed to have met Lawrence; and he discusses the English hero with a deferential reverence that he usually reserves for deities like De Gaulle:

Lawrence, I've met him once. Once only, in a bar of a grand hotel, in Paris, I no longer know which one. We were not equals, you know. He had in his pocket the *Seven Pillars,* his collaboration with Churchill during the peace conference, his rupture with the world and that halo of mystery that the Intelligence Service gave him.

Of course the true mystery was not there. I doubted it without being sure of it at the time. I was a young French writer with only the Prix Goncourt in my pocket. That was little enough. He was extraordinarily elegant. Of an elegance of today, not of his time. A pullover with a rolled neck, a kind of nonchalance and distance.

I don't remember the subjects we discussed. I remember simply that he was then passionate about motors, those of motorcycles and boats. It was a relatively short time before his death. Did he want to die? I have often asked myself that question without being able to answer it.

Unfortunately this statement, so appropriate to Malraux's mythomania, deserves to be true but is patently false. It is significant that on this momentous occasion Malraux, who has a phenomenal memory, does not remember the name of the hotel nor the subjects discussed. Apart from the fact that Lawrence never mentions meeting Malraux, Lawrence did not drink nor frequent the bars of grand hotels; he did not collaborate with Churchill at the Paris Peace Conference of 1919, but at the Cairo Conference of 1921; he had never been in the Intelligence Service, though he did intelligence work for the Arab Bureau in Cairo during 1915–1916; he was not at all elegant, but self-consciously shabby (the pullover with a rolled neck comes from the well-known photograph taken at the end of Lawrence's life and reproduced in the *Letters*); and though Malraux claims to have met Lawrence in Paris after he won the Prix Goncourt in 1933, Lawrence did not leave England between 1933 and his death in 1935. For Malraux the next best thing to actually meeting Lawrence was saying that he had met him.

"As late as 1946 it was rumoured that Malraux was working on studies of [Mayrena] and of T. E. Lawrence whom," writes Frohock, "he thought of as another adventurer of this sort." In the *Antimemoirs* Malraux regrets "There are no real soldiers of fortune left. . . . The myth of Rimbaud is fading"; and he writes at great length about Mayrena, whose legend was still vivid in Indochina during the 1920s and whom Malraux acknowledges as a model for Perken in *The Royal Way* (1930).

Marie-David de Mayrena, an obscure French traveller and soldier, who has been dropped from the more recent editions of *La Grand Encyclopédie,* was compounded in Malraux's imagination of Rajah Brooke, who carved himself the kingdom of Sarawak in Borneo; of Rimbaud, a hopeless adventurer who came to grief in the wilderness of Abyssinia; and of Kurtz in Conrad's *Heart of Darkness* (1899). For like Kurtz, Mayrena was "hot-headed, impulsive, tough and without scruples, and capable of going forward to explore dangerous but useful paths."

The real Mayrena, the son of a captain in the French navy, was born in Toulon in 1842. He accompanied an expedition to Cochin-China in the 1860s, fought in the Franco-Prussian War, took part in missions to Malaysia in the early 1880s, and in 1888 was sent by Constans, the Governor-General of Indochina, to explore the Moi region of the Mekong basin. Mayrena penetrated that unknown territory, formed a confederation with the tribes against their traditional Siamese enemies, forced the wild Mois to recognize his authority and proclaimed himself Marie I, King of the Sedangs. He then ceded political control to France and kept the right of economic exploitation for himself. But when Constans was replaced, the colonial administration quickly lost interest in the Mois and refused to recognize Mayrena's kingdom; and he embarked on an unsuccessful tour of Hong Kong, London and Brussels in search of financial and political support. Frustrated in his ambitions, he abandoned the Mois and retired to the island of Tioman, near Singapore, where he died of a snakebite in 1890.

Conrad's friend, Sir Hugh Clifford, knew Mayrena on Tioman, and described him as an "absurd anachronism," a pretentious and even ludicrous figure who tried to bribe embarrassed colonial officials with colourful but worthless decorations from the Kingdom of the Sedangs. But Malraux, who interpreted Mayrena subjectively and used him for his own purposes, believes "The more Mayrena found himself doomed to obscurity, the more the legend grew. He became very Parisian . . . a disreputable hero, destined less for kingship than for assassination, [but] redeemed by the *feeling he inspired*"—not by the reality of his actions. Malraux quotes Mayrena as complaining, "my enemies take me for an impostor," and comments (in a twice qualified phrase that applies to himself as well as his hero), "Mayrena tells lies. But not all the time, or at least not always undiluted lies."

Like D'Annunzio and Lawrence, Malraux is a talented virtuoso who in the course of his life has been a "book dealer, editor, poet, publisher, explorer, archaeologist, detainee, novelist, reviewer, aviator, revolutionary, politician, orator, soldier, guerrilla leader, minister and philosopher." Malraux's family came from the Dunquerque-Calais region in Flanders. His grandfather was a master-cooper and wine merchant who also owned a fishing fleet that he failed to insure and lost at sea in a storm near Newfoundland. Always incautious, he died by splitting open his own skull with a blow from a double-edged axe. Malraux's father, Fernand, was born in 1879 and married Berthe Lamy, the daughter of a farmer from the Jura, in 1900. Malraux was born in Paris in 1901, and after his parents' separation four years later he grew up and went to school in Bondy, the farthest and greyest of the Paris suburbs, where his mother kept a small grocery store. Malraux's parents were divorced in 1915 and his father, who remarried and moved to Orleans, had two other sons, Roland and Claude. He killed himself in 1930. Though Malraux claimed to have been a student at the Lycée Condorcet and the Ecole des Langues Orientales, there is no record of his enrolment there, and he left school without a diploma. It is not surprising therefore that he states : "Almost all writers I know love their childhood; I hate mine."

Malraux entered the book trade by finding rare volumes on the bookstalls along the Seine and selling them to antiquarian dealers. In 1920 he worked on art books for the publisher Simon Kra, wrote articles for *avant garde* magazines and met artists like Cocteau, Tzara, Artaud, Cendrars, Aragon, Satie and Derain. The following year he published in an expensive limited edition his first book, the Surrealistic fantasy *Lunes en papier* (Paper Moons), and married the wealthy and attractive Jewish intellectual Clara Goldschmidt. Clara relates that "When I used to weep and lament over trifles Malraux would say, 'You are bringing out your little portable wailing wall.' "

The aesthete and idler of the early twenties was very different from the heroic and committed Malraux of subsequent years. He avoided military service with a false medical report and spent the first years of his marriage studying anthropology and oriental art, travelling in Europe and North Africa, and gambling on the stock exchange until he lost all of Clara's money. She records that when "confronted with our economic disaster . . . he simply replied, 'You don't really suppose that I'm going to *work,* do you?'" Instead of work, Malraux planned an expedition to the East that marked the first turning point of his life, for during the twenties his career was dominated by Indochina, just as it was by Spain in the thirties, the Resistance in the forties, art in the fifties and Gaullist politics in the sixties.

During his studies of Khmer art Malraux had read about the once glorious Royal Way in the jungles of Cambodia, and to solve his financial problems the future custodian of French culture decided, as he told Clara, that "We'll go to some little Cambodian temple, we'll take away a few statues, and we'll sell them in America; and that will give us enough to live quietly for two or three years." And Clara adds, "In short, we knew nothing whatever about the country to which we were going, and from it expected everything." This expedition, which turned out disastrously, was thus motivated by a mixture of careful planning and romantic enthusiasm.

Malraux procured some rather vague credentials from the School of Oriental Studies in Paris, and in 1923 sailed for the East with Clara and his friend Louis Chevasson. He made his way to Pnom Penh, and on the strength of his Parisian papers commandeered ox-carts and guides who took him to the Buddhist temple of Banteay-Srey, about forty miles north of Angor Wat. Malraux sawed the sculpture off the temple and loaded it first on the ox-carts and then on the riverboat going to Pnom Penh. The entire adventure in the jungle lasted less than a week, but its sequel was far more protracted. For when they arrived in the capital the police boarded the boat, discovered the stolen statues and arrested Malraux and Chevasson. Malraux remained cool, adopted a cavalier attitude and attributed only slight importance "to an event whose only effect would be the delaying of our plans for a few days."

When Malraux was brought to trial he sent Clara back to France to gather support for him among the intellectuals of Paris, and assumed a perversely contemptuous attitude in court. He "vehemently claimed responsibility for the adventure; sarcasms were directed at the authorities and insults (or words interpreted as such) at the judges." Langlois, in his authoritative account of Malraux's years in Indochina, states that Malraux's lawyer "maintained that no crime had been committed because the ruined Banteay Srei had never been officially classified as an 'historical monument' by the colonial government. Even if it had been, the classification would be invalid because the temple was not under the jurisdiction of that authority." This was the best argument his lawyer could make for a client who had been flagrantly caught with stolen goods, but it was not very convincing and Malraux was condemned to three years in prison. After an appeal in Saigon this was reduced to one year with suspended sentence and was later annulled in Paris. Clara's petition for clemency, which was signed by an impressive number of French writers and artists who admired Malraux's bold but unsuccessful ventures, had been particularly effective. Malraux was fortunate to escape without punishment, and things ended as they began with the adventurer on the loose and the sculpture back in the temple. When the School of Oriental Studies restored Banteay Srey in 1925, the stolen statues were removed from storage in the museum in Pnom Penh and replaced in the temple wall, and unless they were looted or destroyed during the war in Cambodia, they are still there today.

Malraux sailed home in November 1924 swearing vengeance on the dull-witted colonial officials who had subjected him to a humiliating defeat in court. He returned to Saigon the following year, and in June 1925 founded *L'Indochine* with Paul Monin, a liberal lawyer and politician. Their daily, and later weekly, newspaper aggressively supported the nationalistic Young Annam League and crusaded against colonial injustice in a rather bombastic and ineffectual way until it was suppressed by the authorities in February 1926. As Langlois writes:

In spite of his courageous public stand, pessimism eroded Malraux's indomitable spirit during his last two months in Indochina. Weakened by illness, exhausted from the unequal struggle against the ponderous colonial bureaucracy, and somewhat disillusioned by the lack of widespread upper-class Annamite support for his liberal programme, he began to feel that effective reforms in the colony could be initiated only in France.

Malraux had left France as the non-political creator of Surrealistic fantasies; and when he came home (with some hashish for Clara) after his Indochina trial and newspaper career early in 1926, he had been transformed into an extreme opponent of colonialism. Nervous, intense, energetic, and a brilliant talker, with a brooding expression and a cigarette dangling from the side of his mouth in a manner that would soon be adopted by generations of film stars, Malraux was a kind of high-brow Humphrey Bogart, tough but smart. Jean Prévost's description of Malraux in 1926 reveals that the handsome and elegant adventurer, who seemed to have risked death in the jungle, made a powerful impression on his friends :

> He couldn't look you in the eye. His gaze followed an invisible bee in every direction. He would shift his shoulders as if a knife were sticking in his back. A punished child, a tense rebel, who had experienced everything but death, that was Malraux on his return from Asia. He tried to shield himself from others and from things behind polite forms, doctrines, crazy fantasies. Pen in hand he flayed at life. His genius could deal with it. Action more than years made him a man. Danger had given his heart muscle.

And in that same year Maurice Sachs was overwhelmed by the qualities that Malraux shared with Lawrence : adventurousness, will-power and intelligence :

> I've met Malraux. He makes a vivid impression. In his look he has the air of adventure, of melancholy and of irresistible will-power, a fine profile of a Renaissance Italian, and yet a very French appearance. He speaks very fast, very well, with the air of knowing everything, dazzles you with his self-confidence and leaves you with the impression that you've met the most intelligent man of the century.

In 1926 Malraux published *The Temptation of the West,* a cultural dialogue between an occidental in Asia and an oriental in Europe which, influenced by Spengler's *Decline of the West* (1918, 1922), attacked colonialism indirectly by celebrating the superiority of Eastern civilization. In 1928 he brought out his first novel, *The Conquerors,* which describes the failure of the 1925 insurrection in Canton, the headquarters of the Kuomintang (the Chinese Nationalist Government). In a letter of 1929 Malraux explains how this novel formulates one of the major concerns in his work : "The fundamental question for Garine is much less how to participate in revolution than how to escape what he calls the absurd. The whole of *The Conquerors* is a perpetual quest, and I have moreover insisted on the phrase : to escape the idea of the absurd by seeking refuge in what is human."

Malraux had made a brief trip from Saigon to Hong Kong to purchase type for *L'Indochine* at the time of the nationalist rising in Canton; and in a famous letter to Edmund Wilson in 1933, Malraux said that he organized the Young Annam movement in Saigon and then became *commissaire* in charge of propaganda and information for the Kuomintang, first in Indochina (1924) and then in Canton (1925). Though Malraux was in Hong Kong for a few days in the latter part of 1925, he did *not* go to Canton during the insurrection; and there is absolutely no evidence to substantiate his claim to political power. It is therefore ironic that during Malraux's dispute with Trotsky about the ideology of *The Conquerors,* the self-styled *commissaire,* who supposedly served the Comintern and the Kuomintang in 1925, was accused by the revolutionary hero of "carrying responsibility for the strangulation of the Chinese revolution."

In 1928, the year of *The Conquerors,* Malraux purged himself of his last Surrealistic fantasy, *Royaume farfelu* (Crazy Kingdom), and joined the publisher Gallimard as an editor of art books and organizer of exhibitions. Gallimard also published the distinguished journal *Nouvelle Revue Française,* whose leading contributor André Gide soon became Malraux's close friend. Maurice Sachs, who recognized the fraudulent D'Annunzian element in Malraux's genius, writes :

The figure who made the greatest effect at the *NRF* was André Malraux, and he had dazzling qualities : a uniquely lively and agile intelligence, a fine voice, a warm and persuasive manner of speaking, an admirable face, though it was beginning to be spoiled by the many tics he could not control or get rid of, elegant in everything, in his bearing, in his manner, in the gestures of his very beautiful hands, and besides his understanding, his attention, his curiosity, much generosity. And yet a bit of a charlatan! He seemed false because he believed that to be less than everything is to be nothing. And yet one could not know him without growing fond of a being so courageous, coldly heroic, passionate with almost as much impartiality as one could find in passion, compassionate, helpful, the friend of suffering mankind, yet not very human, too rational, sometimes crazy, never ordinary and all the same fairly *farfelu*. He never took me seriously and I do not know if that made me see that there was an element of farce in his seriousness, of superficiality in his knowledge, but something fine and lovable in his whole being.

During 1929–1931 Malraux, always an enthusiastic traveller, visited Persia, Afghanistan, India, Malaya and China (the setting of *Man's Fate*) and studied the masterpieces of Eastern art, one of the dominant interests of his life. In 1930 he published *The Royal Way*, a fascinating and under-rated novel about a search for sculpture in the jungle, which was based on his experience in Cambodia, inspired by the heroic adventurer Mayrena and strongly influenced by the dark fate of Kurtz in *Heart of Darkness*.

In 1933 Malraux won the Prix Goncourt, France's most important literary award, for *Man's Fate*. Malraux's greatest novel, which describes Chiang Kai-shek's destruction of his former Communist allies in Shanghai in 1927, concerns the conflict of mind and will and the possibilities of transcending Pascal's concept of the human condition: Gisors with opium and Katov with self-sacrifice, Chen through assassination and Kyo through suicide, Clappique in gambling and Ferral in eroticism. Malraux's portrayal of Ferral and Valerie is a brilliant and sophisticated analysis of the relationship between love, freedom and power that is also reflected in the marriage of Kyo and May, whose betrayal of her husband is based on Clara's confession of infidelity on her voyage from Indochina to France. As in Conrad's *Victory* and Camus' *The Plague*, which are ideologically close to Malraux, the tragic victory of the defeated men (Chen, Katov and Kyo, who was modelled on Chou En-lai) is far more meaningful than the fate of those who survive the abortive insurrection (Clappique, Ferral and Gisors). Though Malraux's ideas evolve from his portrayal of revolutionary politics, his dominant theme, the affirmation of man's dignity and grandeur in tragic defeat, has two serious limitations. The opiate withdrawal and reflective wisdom of old Gisors diminishes the mode of action in the novel, and the ultimate transcendence and dignity are achieved only at the moment of death and with no hope of social amelioration. Zarathustra's answer is also Malraux's: "Die at the right time. He that consummates his life dies his death victoriously, surrounded by those who hope and promise."

The royalties from the vast sales of *Man's Fate,* which inevitably followed the award of the Prix Goncourt, financed Malraux's next *farfelu* adventure, his flight over the Arabian desert in 1934 (it was too dangerous to land in that wild territory) in order to discover the Queen of Sheba's city. The flight was as bizarre as the great jungle robbery and as fantastic as his plan to rescue Trotsky from exile in remote Alma Ata, and it furnished an abundance of mythomanic material.

Malraux's imagination was stimulated by a number of sources and models. The first Book of Kings relates how the fabulously wealthy Queen of Sheba "came to Jerusalem with a very great train, with camels that bare spices, and very much gold, and precious stones : and when she was come to Solomon, she communed with him of all that was in her heart." And Malraux wrote in 1934 that Sheba's ruined city, which had decayed before the rise of Islam in the seventh century, was an "immense petrifaction still filled—beneath the five kilometres of its livid marble—with the dreams of millions of men, and the deaths of a few." In the *Natural History* Pliny describes the sixty glorious temples of the Queen; and Sheba appears as an apparition to tempt Flaubert's St. Anthony. Though a stranger in a Djibouti hotel once confided to Malraux "that somewhere beyond the Yemen desert, half hidden by the sand, the real capital of the Queen of Sheba still stands," the most powerful and direct inspiration came from Rimbaud's and Lawrence's penetration of the forbidden deserts of Abyssinia and Arabia.

Only the demands of a recent marriage prevented Saint-Exupéry from piloting Malraux, who boldly announced his search in the *Nouvelles littéraires.* In the beginning of March 1934 Malraux set out in a single engine plane with his friend Corniglion-Molinier on a ten-hour non-stop flight of 1250 miles from Djibouti in French Somaliland to the Arabian desert, and back again. And on March 10th Malraux cabled *L'Intransigeant,* a Paris newspaper with a strong interest in aviation that had commissioned Malraux to write about his expedition : "Have discovered legendary city of Queen of Sheba. 20 towers or temples still standing. Is *north* of Rub' al Khali [the Empty Quarter]. Have taken photos for Intransigeant. Greetings. Corniglion-Malraux."

This astonishing news was elaborated in a series of ten articles (seven by Malraux and three by Corniglion), "Au-dessus du désert d'Arabie," which appeared in the newspaper between May 3rd and May 13th, 1934. Like D'Annunzio's flight over Vienna, Malraux's flight over

Arabia was clearly a publicity stunt; and Malraux had to produce a good newspaper story to justify the expenses and the risks of the journey. He knew that he was free to say whatever he liked as there was no way to verify his account and almost impossible to prove it was false.

Malraux begins with a good deal of potted history, based mainly on rumour and myth, and ends with his post-flight reception at the royal court of Ethiopia, whose king was the putative descendant of the great Queen. The crux of the story is presented by Malraux on May 9th when he relates that they flew over the city of Saba (Sheba), for which he gives no latitudinal or longitudinal bearings; that the Bedouins fired muskets at the low-flying plane; and that the mysterious city was "like an enormous monument, like the towers of Notre Dame . . . blind towers . . . trapezoid towers . . . vast terraces . . . propylaea . . . walls 40 metres high . . . broken statues." To corroborate this marvellous description the newspaper published Malraux's large but indistinct photograph, blurred by the dust of the desert, that does not correspond to his verbal description and looks more like an ordinary Bedouin village than a ruined city.

Janet Flanner, who has followed the scholarly controversy provoked by Malraux's assertions, reports that the French Orientalist, Jules Barthoux, said that "Malraux had consulted with him about Sheba's city in 1930 but what he had just flown over was unfortunately a ruin called Wabar, the Arabic name for some large rodents that lived in its rocks." But Wabar is in the middle of the Empty Quarter about 600 miles northeast of Sana, and in *Arabia Felix* (1932) the explorer Bertram Thomas states that "today it is an untrodden desert owing to the drying up of its water. There are to be found in it great buildings which the wind has smothered in sand"—and which would *not* be visible from the air. Flanner then quotes the opinion of another expert :

> The University of Pennsylvania's Professor of Assyriology said, also in the *Herald Tribune,* that Malraux had undoubtedly found some-body's ruined city, but not Sheba's, which was authoritatively believed to be in the south of Arabia Felix, at Marib—a well-known theory, which, for some reason, Malraux refused to subscribe to; though in his flight, he passed over Marib to take a peek at it, out of curiosity, and later reported that he thought it small.

Malraux, like Lawrence, frequently provides more than one version of the crucial events of his life, and his account of the flight over Sheba in *Antimemoirs* contradicts the sensational articles in *L'Intransigeant*. In 1934, as we have seen, Malraux claimed to have flown over Saba and seen 20 towers and walls 40 metres high; in 1967 he claims to have flown over Mareb and seen massive ramparts, horse-shoe walls and cuboid buildings. Both Saba and Mareb are *south,* not north of the Empty Quarter, as Malraux claimed in his original cable to the newspaper (see map). In any case, the distance from Sana in the south (which Malraux recognized from the air by its fort) to Harad, the first village north of the Empty Quarter, is about 700 miles, or $2\frac{1}{2}$ times farther than the minimum direct distance from Djibouti to Sana (275 miles). So it was clearly impossible for Malraux, who states that he flew for 5 hours at a maximum speed of 130 miles per hour (*Antimemoirs*, p. 70), to reach either Wabar or a site north of the Empty Quarter, which would be about 900–1000 miles from Djibouti.

Langlois, a scholar devoted to Malraux in more than one sense, has attempted to explain away one contradiction in Malraux's two accounts: "To simplify the narrative in *Antimemoirs* Malraux speaks of Mareb as the goal of the expedition, but the site actually sought—and found— was an unnamed ruin some 100 miles to the north." This statement presents two serious difficulties. First Malraux never attempts to simplify the extremely complex narrative of *Antimemoirs*, which constantly shifts backwards and forwards in time and has an almost Jamesian impenetrability. Second, if the vague "unnamed ruin" which Langlois believes Malraux actually found were 100 miles north of Mareb, it would be (like Wabar) *inside* the completely uninhabited Empty Quarter. Yet in both accounts Malraux states that he was prevented from landing near the village because the Bedouin fired rifles at his low-flying airplane. (In *Seven Pillars of Wisdom* Lawrence relates how *his* Bedouin soldiers fled in terror the first time they saw a Turkish airplane.) Therefore, Malraux must have changed the name of the ruins he claimed to discover in order to confuse matters and make it more difficult to prove precisely what he did or did not find. It is also possible that after rejecting in 1934 the authoritative theory that Mareb was in fact ancient Sheba, he then did more reading, became convinced that Mareb *was* Sheba and decided that if there were any ruins to be found they would *have* to be found in Mareb.

In the *Antimemoirs* version Malraux states that "The ruins of Mareb, the ancient Saba or Sheba, lie in the Hadhramaut [a district of southern

Arabia, on the Arabian Sea], *south* of the desert, north-west of Aden";
and he mentions the well-known legend of the rat who loosened a stone
of the Mareb dam, which then burst open and destroyed the Kingdom
of Sheba. Malraux also refers to the explorers who died in their attempt
to reach Mareb by land, and he quotes Arnaud, another of the admired
breed of vanished adventurers, who declared: "Leaving Mareb, I
visited the ruins of ancient Sheba, which in general have nothing to
show but mounds of earth." (In the *Journal Asiatique* for 1845 Thomas
Joseph Arnaud had reported: "Not a trace of a building is to be seen,
not a single large stone to be found.") But Malraux is undaunted by
Arnaud's denial and makes no attempt to reconcile the contradiction
between Arnaud's statement and his own rich description. In the crucial
passage of *Antimemoirs,* which as we have seen is entirely different from
his description of 1934, Malraux declares that when he flew over Mareb
90 years after Arnaud had been there, he saw

> the ruins encroach on the desert. Those massive oval ramparts, whose
> debris was clearly visible against the soil, could they be temples?
> How to make a landing? To one side lay the dunes, in which the
> plane would overturn; to the other, a volcanic soil with rocks pro-
> jecting from the sand. Closer to the ruins, the ground was caved in
> everywhere. We flew still lower, and went on photographing. The
> horse-shoe walls opened on empty space: the town, built of sun-dried
> bricks like Nineveh, must have similarly reverted to the desert. We
> turned back to the main mass: an oval tower, more ramparts, cuboid
> buildings. Tiny flames flickered against the dark patches of Bedouin
> tents scattered outside the ruins. They must be firing at us. On the
> other side of the walls we begin to make out the mysterious traces of
> things whose purpose we could not fathom. The flat H on the tower
> overlooking the ruins, what did it represent? Part of an observatory?

Malraux concludes, rather vaguely, by remarking that "Sheba, or
Mareb, whatever one likes to call it, is still in the hands of the [Bedouin]
dissidents. . . . One day, perhaps, a scientific expedition from independent
Aden will clear up 'the mystery of Sheba.' "

Malraux would be surprised to find that this mystery had been cleared
up as early as 1936, only two years after his flight, when St. John
Philby, father of the notorious spy, political rival of Lawrence, convert
to Islam, friend of King Saud of Saudi Arabia, and one of the greatest

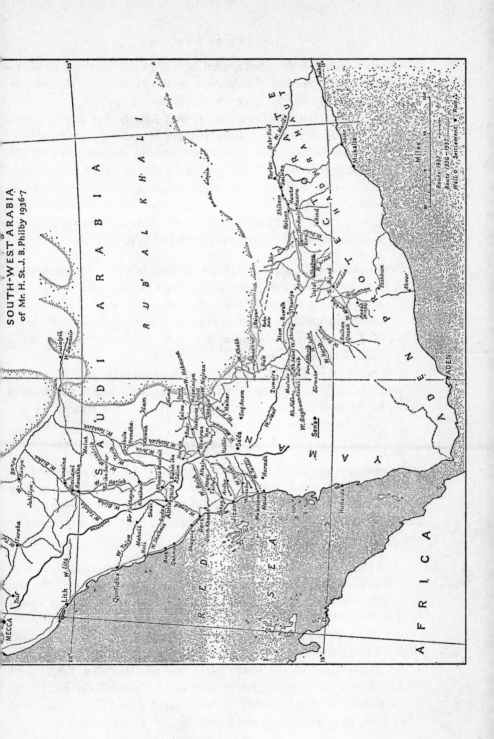

SOUTH-WEST ARABIA
of Mr. H. St. J. B. Philby 1936-7

Route 1932
Route 1936-1937
Well ○ ; Settlement ●   Ruin ∴

Miles
0   50   100

modern explorers of the desert, went by car to examine and to photograph "the only piece of the Arabian peninsula that was entirely un-
explored." (Philby either ignores or is unaware of Arnaud.)

Philby visited both Shabwa (Saba) and Mareb (the transliteration
from the Arabic accounts for the difference in spelling), which are 115
miles apart and which Malraux claimed to have discovered in his first
and in his second versions. Philby provides a plan of the original *founda-
tions* of the ruins of Shabwa (190 miles east of Sana), but his photographs merely show some piles of rocks. Pliny's *Natural History* had
also aroused Philby's archaeological expectations and he reports with
some irritation in the *Geographical Journal* of 1938 that

> Pliny's account of Shabwa . . . is grossly inaccurate. As for the number
> of its temples, there could never have been 60 nor even 6 within the
> exiguous space enclosed by the city walls. One outstanding temple
> of supreme magnificence it certainly had, and two other ruin heaps
> within the walls may also some day prove to be temples. But 3 is a
> very different matter from 60.
> The whole ruin-field lay before us, disappointingly small and insig-
> nificant. . . . Not a single ancient building stood intact, not a pillar
> of the 60 temples erect. The ancient capital of the Himyarites was
> just a jumble of fallen debris.

It was considerably more difficult and dangerous to inspect Mareb (85
miles east of Sana) for the Imam of Yemen forbade all visitors and the
inhabitants were openly hostile. But Philby, who ventured close enough
to study the village with binoculars, did *not* find massive ramparts, oval
towers, cuboid buildings and observatories in Mareb any more than he
did in Shabwa.

> I did pay a flying visit to the threshold of the Sheban capital, Marib.
> It was a rather risky experiment as it had to be done hurriedly and
> secretly with a single car and only two guides. . . . The town or village
> of modern Marib stands on a low hillock and appeared in the distance,
> as I saw it through my glasses, as a group of buildings occupying the
> slopes and summit of the hill and forming a fine silhouette against the
> dull background of the sandy plain beyond. Doubtless the ancient
> capital occupied a much larger area around the hillock, but it was
> not possible to make out any of the detail. I should like to have had
> a nearer view, but in the circumstances that was impossible.

Janet Flanner believes that Malraux flew "over a majestic archaeological ruin in Arabia Felix [Yemen] which was, after all, apparently *not* Sheba's city." Langlois is even more credulous, accepts Malraux at his own valuation, and concludes with a lyrical but totally unrealistic series of abstractions that are meant to explain the significance of Malraux's search for Sheba's city: the Sabaean adventure "permitted Malraux simultaneously to act and to prove his existence as a man, to dream under the stimulus of that action, and to record his poetic *cortège de rêves*. [Malraux could have done all this in bed in Paris.] In retrospect it also furnished him with a certain deepened metaphysical awareness."

Langlois also links the Sabaean with the Cambodian adventure and confidently concedes: "Malraux knew that only hard facts would silence those who were attacking him (as they had done once before after his return from the jungles of Cambodia) as an irresponsible adventurer or a fraud." We have seen that Malraux could not possibly have flown to a village *north* of the Empty Quarter, Bertram Thomas stated there were no visible ruins at Wabar and Philby provides the "hard facts" that "clear up the mystery of Sheba." His descriptions prove that there were not 20 nor even 2 "towers or temples still standing" at Saba, as Malraux claimed in 1934 when he reduced Pliny's number by two-thirds. And Philby also confirms Arnaud's statement, quoted by Malraux himself, that there was "nothing to show but mounds of earth." We must therefore conclude that in the flight over the Arabian desert Malraux was not only an irresponsible adventurer but also a fraud.

It would be more profitable, however, to attempt to understand Malraux's motives than to admire or condemn him, for as he says in the *Antimemoirs,* "To know a man nowadays is above all to know the element of the irrational in him, the part he is unable to control." Having announced with considerable publicity and fanfare that he was about to undertake a flamboyant and heroic adventure, Malraux, who did not want to spoil the glorious opportunity by returning with a handful of dust, felt obliged to discover something spectacular. Given his predisposition to mythomania (that is, lies), his unwillingness to disappoint either his own expectations or those of his newspaper audience, and the impossibility of refuting or verifying the facts of his story, Malraux had virtually no choice but to invent an exciting and imaginative alternative to the dull reality of the empty desert—he owed this much to the Bible, to Pliny and to Flaubert. By the time of the *Antimemoirs* (not conventional, but selective and highly embellished memoirs) the search for Sheba, which had hardened into a legend that was impossible to deny, provided the ideal quest for the romantic adventurer. So Malraux brought the archaeological theory up to date, switched to Mareb, and heightened and shaped the exotic story until it fit in to the pattern of his fictionalized autobiography. Malraux flew over Arabia not to discover Sheba's city, but to realize his fantasies and create a legendary *persona* worthy of Lawrence and Rimbaud.

After 1933, when *Man's Fate* was published and Hitler took power, Malraux became a deeply committed anti-fascist and a powerful spokesman for the Left. His flight over Arabia took place between January 1934 when he made an unsuccessful trip to Berlin with Gide to demand the release of the Bulgarian Dimitrov, who had been falsely imprisoned for starting the Reichstag fire, and the summer of 1934 when he attended the Congress of Writers in Moscow. Malraux, who awed Gide with "his dazzling and staggering flow of words" and who impressed Spender as "the most brilliant and dynamic conversationalist I had met," dominated the 1935 Congress of Writers in Paris, which was attended by Forster, Huxley, Gide, Martin du Gard, Aragon and Ehrenburg. In that year Malraux published his fourth novel, *Days of Wrath,* which dealt with conditions inside the Nazi concentration camps and created that atmosphere of psychological stress that was later portrayed in the political novels of Silone, Koestler and Orwell.

There is a considerable difference between Malraux's political crusading in Indochina and his profound commitment in Spain. In July 1936, two days after the outbreak of the Civil War that began like the October Revolution, with cinemas open and visitors strolling in the streets, Malraux, internationally famous as a Left-wing writer, arrived in Madrid. He immediately began to buy aircraft—often outdated and delapidated —for the Rupublican Government, and to recruit mercenaries—who were paid fifty thousand francs a month—for his flying squadron of volunteers.

Malraux's headquarters in Madrid was the Hotel Florida on the Gran Via where Hemingway and Dos Passos, Pablo Neruda and Rafael Alberti, and the Russian journalists Mikhail Koltzov and Ilya Ehrenburg often met. The latter describes Malraux in Spain as

a man who is always in the grip of a single absorbing passion. I knew him during the period of his infatuation with the East, then with

Dostoyevsky and Faulkner, then with the brotherhood of workers and the revolution. In Valencia he thought and spoke only about the bombing of fascist positions and when I started to say something about literature, he twitched and fell silent.

Malraux, who was not a Communist, saw the Party "not as a means of persuasion but as a means of action"; and even before the Communists decided to form the International Brigade, he organized the Escadre España (the international air force) and commanded it with boldness and courage. He flew on 65 missions as a bombardier and gunner, and was wounded during a raid, which led Hemingway to remark that Malraux must have acquired his tic at well over 10,000 feet.

The first battle of Malraux's squadron, which provided moral as well as military support, took place in August 1936 at Medellín, the birth-place of Cortez in Estremadura, when six planes flying low enough to fire pistols destroyed a motorized column of Franco's forces. In December 1936 during a bombing raid on Teruel, northwest of Valencia, Malraux's antiquated planes fought bravely against the modern Nazi Heinkels. An episode in this battle provided the moving and vivid image of human fraternity that Malraux used both in *Man's Hope* and in his film, *L'Espoir*. During his political tour of America in 1937 Malraux described how

On December 27 one of the planes of my squadron was brought down in the Teruel region—behind our lines. It had fallen very high, at about 2,000 metres above sea level, and snow covered the mountains. In this region there are very few villages, and it was only after several hours that the peasants arrived and began constructing stretchers for the wounded and a coffin for the dead. When all was ready the descent began . . . [Later] I raised my eyes: the file of peasants extended now from the heights of the mountain to its base—and it was the grandest image of fraternity I have ever encountered.

The Escadre España fought at Toledo, Madrid, Jarama and at Guada-lajara, the headquarters of the Russian air squadron northeast of the capital, where in March 1937 they bombed the Italian troops who were eventually defeated in battle. After Guadalajara Malraux's patched-up and punished planes literally fell apart after seven months of combat, and the squadron was replaced by a more professional and modern air force.

Malraux had separated from Clara (who refused to divorce him) in 1936, three years after the birth of their daughter Florence; and when he visited New York and Los Angeles, Harvard, Princeton and Berkeley in March 1937 to raise funds for the Loyalist cause, he was accompanied by Josette Clotis. Armand Petitjean, who heard Malraux speak at a Loyalist rally in France, describes the inspiring effect of Malraux's speech, which seemed to embody the highest values of humanity:

> I must admit that it was magnificent. Never in my life have I seen such self-mastery, such power of a man, of *homo loquens,* of the man himself over other men. Malraux, I did not like you overmuch, but when you spoke, not for us in the hall but for those in the trenches, you gave us some idea of human greatness. And the proof is that it was not you we were applauding, but Spain.

During the next two years of the Civil War Malraux moved from action to art, published *Man's Hope* (1937) and wrote and directed *L'Espoir* (1938), which was based on certain episodes in the novel. During an interview in 1970 Malraux said, "I believe myself that the Spanish Revolution was the last great expression of hope," the Second World War brought what he called "the return of Satan." Though Malraux considers *Man's Hope* his greatest achievement, this novel, which attempts to combine reportage, propaganda and ideology with a fictional account of Malraux's experience of contemporary history, is more ambitious but certainly less successful than *Man's Fate*. For the lengthy philosophical discussions about art, politics and heroism, faith, death and the apocalyptic vision, are not well integrated into the violent and episodic events of the book. As Gide observed of Malraux's novels, "The excessive use of abstract terms is often prejudicial to the narration of the action. One must not try simultaneously to make the reader visualize and to make him understand." Malraux's characters do not always embody his thematic abstractions, and Hernandez's philosophical refusal to save himself when another prisoner cuts the rope that binds them remains unconvincing in the context of the action.

The triumphant affirmation of the novel was extremely effective as Loyalist propaganda. Malraux writes about the siege of the Alcazar in Toledo in 1936 as if the fascists were about to surrender when, in fact, a supporting force broke through the Republican defences around the city, rescued the fortress and achieved a legendary victory. Malraux was also excellent in conveying the heroic spirit of men in war; and the famous descent from the mountain, inspired by the plane crash at Teruel, became the poignant finale of the film and of the novel:

> It had begun to drizzle. The last stretchers, the peasants from the mountains, and the last mules were advancing between the vast background of the rocky landscape over which the dark rain-clouds were massing, and the hundreds of peasants standing motionless with raised fists. The women were weeping quietly, and the procession seemed to be fleeing from the eerie silence of the mountains, its noise of clattering hoofs and clogs linking the everlasting clamour of the vultures with the muffled sound of sobbing.

Malraux filmed *L'Espoir* in Barcelona during the war while the city was constantly under attack by enemy bombers based on Majorca. *L'Espoir* was influenced by the cinematic realism of Eisenstein and foreshadows post-war films by Rossellini and De Sica. Its many outdoor sequences convey a vivid feeling of what Spain was like during the Civil War and how the Republicans fought with insufficient and obsolete equipment. The film is both subtle and persuasive as propaganda, moving and meaningful as art; it is a tribute to the foreign fighters in Spain and portrays the values and ideals of the Republicans. Its greatest scenes are the destruction of a strategic piece of artillery by a suicidal car driver, the peasant's initial failure to recognize his village and identify an enemy airfield from a plane, and the procession of the wounded aviators from the mountain. *L'Espoir* is a truly extraordinary achievement since Malraux had no previous film experience, shot the film in the midst of the Civil War and grasped the significance of the historical events that he portrayed just after they had occurred. James Agee rightly calls *L'Espoir* "one of the few wonderful film records of men in courage and sorrow. . . . Homer might know it, I think, for the one work of our time which was wholly sympathetic to him." Ironically, when Malraux left Spain in January 1939 to complete in the French Pyrenees the film that celebrates the glories of the Loyalist struggle, Franco's army was approaching Barcelona and the war was all but lost.

Malraux's military and artistic achievements during the Second World War equalled his record in Spain. Early in the war he enlisted as a private in the Tank Corps and was captured with his unit during the fall of France. But in November 1940 he put on carpenter's overalls, carried a plank on his shoulder and walked out of the prisoner of war camp at Sens. He made his way to the Unoccupied Zone, joined Josette and her family in the south of France, and temporarily opted out of the war. Sartre "found him living in lordly style in a villa at Saint-Jean Cap-Ferrat," where he was writing *The Walnut Trees of Altenburg,* published in Switzerland in 1943. This superb novel contains the greatest scene in Malraux's fiction: a description of how in the Great War the victorious Germans, horrified at the success of their gas attack when they personally confront their Russian victims, wearily carry the suffering enemy back to the healing safety of their own lines. As Malraux writes of his hero, Vincent Berger, "What he liked about war was the masculine comradeship, the irrevocable commitments that courage imposes."

Under the name of "Colonel Berger" Malraux became active in the Resistance in the spring of 1944 and commanded 1500 *maquis* in the Dordogne region of southwest France. In the *Antimemoirs* and again in his commemorative speech on the Resistance leader Jean Moulin, in *Oraisons funèbres,* Malraux recalls a silent and symbolic incident from this period that reveals the same striking visual image of man in nature, and the same tribute to heroism and human solidarity, as in the descent from the mountain in Teruel:

> I thought, too, of the dawn rising over a cemetery in Corrèze surrounded by woods white with hoar-frost. The Germans had shot some maquisards, and the inhabitants were to bury them in the morning. A company had occupied the cemetery, sub-machine-guns at the ready. In that region, the women do not follow the hearse, they wait for it beside the family grave. At day-break, on each of the tombs on the hillside like the scattered stones of ancient amphitheatres, a woman in black could be seen standing, and not praying.

On D-Day in June the elite SS Division *Das Reich* was sent north to reinforce the defences at Normandy and Malraux was ordered to retard their progress. Cookridge reports that on June 7th Malraux's *maquis*

> went into action. In a series of ambushes and skirmishes, the long German tank columns were halted and forced to abandon the main road. . . . The Division arrived in Normandy ten days behind schedule,

completely disorganized, leaving many disabled tanks behind with its men hardly able to fight.

In July 1944, four months after he joined the *maquis*, Malraux's driver was killed as their car overturned during an ambush by an SS platoon. Malraux escaped from the car, was shot in the right leg, captured and sent to St. Michel prison in Toulouse. During his interrogation he justified the Resistance movement by telling the German officer : "Every struggle presupposes a soul. . . . In 1940 France suffered one of the most appalling defeats in her history. Those who are fighting you are guarantors of her survival." Like Dostoyevsky, Malraux was also placed before a firing squad in a mock execution, and his description of this traumatic event in *Antimemoirs* is strongly influenced by the autobiographical passages in *The Idiot*. Malraux escaped torture only because his dossier failed to arrive from Gestapo headquarters, and he was freed from prison when the Germans abandoned Toulouse in September.

Malraux commanded the Alsace-Lorraine Brigade under General Le Clerc from September 1944 until February 1945, and took part in the capture of Dannemarie in November, the defence of Strasbourg against von Runstedt's offensive in December, the march on Colmar and Sainte-Odilie, and the triumphant entry into Strasbourg. Malraux received the Croix de la Libération and the Croix de Guerre with four citations for his distinguished service; but he had suffered great personal losses in the war. Both his half-brothers, Roland and Claude, had been killed; and Josette Clotis, who had borne him two sons, Gauthier and Vincent, was crushed and killed when she fell under a train in November 1944. It is hardly surprising therefore that just after the war C. L. Sulzberger found Malraux "extremely nervous and rather dissipated looking : very thin, with dark shadows under his eyes and a long nose and face. He smokes American cigarettes constantly and refuses to sit down, walking about all the time . . . He was constantly at an extreme point of tension."

One rather naive literary critic has been puzzled about the last phase of Malraux's life and "cannot help wondering why the author of *La Condition Humaine* preferred to deliver funeral orations and organize exhibitions (however splendid) rather than to pursue his own novelistic work." But the answer is obvious. Malraux, who had spent his life fighting for the underdog against superior forces and had invented his role of authority in the Kuomintang, wanted to have political power and to become one of those figures around whom history prowls; he wanted to control the government in order to translate his ideas into reality rather than into art.

In 1945 Malraux, to the surprise and horror of his Left-wing admirers, accepted the Ministry of Information in De Gaulle's short-lived provisional government, and became the leading propagandist for De Gaulle's Right-wing party, the Rassemblement du Peuple Français. A number of scholars, notably Janine Mossuz, have attempted to reconcile Malraux's Gaullism with his pre-war politics. But this task is impossible unless, like Mossuz, one defines the policies of Gaullism either as a tautology ("a faith in the future of another world which only Charles De Gaulle is able to construct") or as a synthesis of *Malraux*'s, but not De Gaulle's, ideas. For Malraux, writes Mossuz, Gaullism "is not uniquely political but metaphysical, and is directed against an adversary, death, and against the train of certainties that accompany it : evil, oppression, servitude, chains of all sorts"—though one could argue that these "certainties" accompany life and are extinguished by death.

Boak, who maintains a healthy scepticism about Malraux's career, is much closer to the truth when he places Malraux within the French literary-political tradition and states that it seems pointless to claim "his political attitude has never basically changed . . . Communism and Gaullism have little in common except their authoritarian approach. . . . Certainly Malraux has moved sharply from Left to Right in politics : but this has been, especially in France, so common a development among writers as to be almost typical." Malraux himself has admitted in an illuminating remark of 1969, "There *is* a gap between my present views and the ideas of my youth . . . I have replaced the proletariat by France". And he has rather subjectively defined Gaullism as "political passion in the service of France."

Malraux, like so many other disillusioned intellectuals on the Left, became hostile to "the God that failed" after the Stalinist Purge Trials of the late 1930s, which eliminated virtually all the Russians who had served in Spain. Malraux equates Gaullism with anti-Communism and writes that after the war "any movement born of the Resistance must be Gaullist if it did not want to be communist : because only the General was really prepared to set up an independent State and nation as an alternative to a communist State." Though Malraux has denied

with unusual modesty that De Gaulle said to him what Napoleon said
when first introduced to Goethe ("Voilà, l'homme!"), the General has
lavished pompous praise on his Minister :

> On my right, then as always, was André Malraux. The presence at
> my side of this inspired friend, this devotee of lofty doctrines, gave
> me a sense of being insured against the commonplace. The conception
> which this incomparable witness to our age had formed of me did
> much to fortify me. I know that in debate, when the subject was
> grave, his flashing judgments would help to dispel the shadows.

In the *Antimemoirs* Malraux quotes his remark to De Gaulle that the
Resistance led some "towards revolutionary romanticism, which consists
in confusing political action with theatre." This extremely revealing
remark is a perfect definition both of Malraux's direction of the Rassemblement's tasteless D'Annunzian-style rallies, which were held in the
Paris Vélodrome (the six-day bike race stadium) during the late 1940s,
and of his career as a Gaullist Minister when he disguised the authoritarian politics of the Fifth Republic with a stream of theatrical oratory.
Lacouture, who witnessed the political sound and light spectacles of the
Rassemblement, writes that there were "projectors, platforms, water-
works, backdrops, music : for three years Charles De Gaulle was a giant
Gallic druid . . . with an invincible silhouette and a resounding voice—
floodlit and recorded in stereophonic sound by the producer of *L'Espoir*."
The later speeches in *Oraisons funèbres* "give the impression of an orator
of the seventeenth century who had dreamed of Lautréamont and studied
diction with Sarah Bernhardt," says Lacouture. But the orator of the
post-war Rassemblement has

> nothing written. No plan. Some telling phrases—heroic slogans or
> fine words—serve as the *leitmotiv* of this discourse. With these
> ideas in his head he begins to expound the parallels between
> Goya and the Grand Turk, between the Marquis de Sade and
> Maurice Thorez, between the cathedrals and the slaughterhouses of
> Chicago, or between De Gaulle and François I.

Though few people in the enormous crowd could follow the dazzling
flow of words that had once awed André Gide, Flanner confirms that
Malraux created a tremendous, if confusing, impression :

He made what was undoubtedly the most exciting, excitable speech, feverishly kneading his hands, as in his platform habit, extinguishing his voice with passion and reviving it with gulps of water, and presenting an astonishing exposition of politico-aesthetics that seemed like fireworks shot from the head of a statue.

Though successful as theatre, these rallies were useless as practical politics, and the Rassemblement collapsed of *hubris*, gigantism and inertia in 1952.

After the war Malraux resumed his passionate study not only of Eastern art but also of his favourite painters—Rembrandt, Vermeer, Goya and Braque—a study that had been reflected in the serious discussions of aesthetic questions in both *The Royal Way* and *Man's Hope*. The results of his lifelong interest in art were published in the lavishly illustrated *Voices of Silence* (1951), *The Imaginary Museum* (1952-54), and *The Metamorphosis of the Gods* (1957), immensely long and complex yet intuitive and personal books, which suggest a cultural synthesis and unity in all works of art. Though received coldly by academic art historians, Malraux's unique and original work reveals a characteristic breadth of scope and range of learning, and is highly suggestive and stimulating.

When De Gaulle returned to power in June 1958, Malraux became his Minister of Cultural Affairs, and attempted to implement a number of political and aesthetic programmes. During the Algerian crisis in 1958 Malraux had the idea of sending the three French Nobel Prize winners, Martin du Gard, Mauriac and Camus, to Algiers "as a kind of permanent ambassador of the French conscience in the name of De Gaulle." But this project was never realized, perhaps because Camus preferred to retain and represent his own conscience. Malraux believed "The only thing we can save [in the colonies] is a kind of cultural empire, a domain of [French] values"; and he helped to enforce the policy of decolonization, proclaimed the independence of four new African states, and was nearly murdered during the Algerian war of 1962 by Right-wing extremists who opposed the policy of De Gaulle.

As Minister of Cultural Affairs he continued to travel extensively and to represent France in countries throughout the world. He restored palaces, cleaned the façades of buildings and transformed the appearance of Paris. He directed art exhibitions and reorganized the National

Theatres; and dismissed the popular Jean-Louis Barrault, the director of the Odéon Theatre, for openly sympathizing with the students during the May Revolution of 1968. And in a programme that recalled the Soviet projects of the 1930s, he created Houses of Culture in some provincial cities.

While he was a Minister, in 1961, Malraux's two sons, like their mother, were killed in a violent accident. In 1965 Malraux separated from his second wife, Madeleine, the widow of his half-brother Roland, whom he had married in 1948. And in the summer of that year, after a serious illness, he took a recuperative sea voyage to Egypt, India and China. In Peking the Right-wing Minister and connoisseur of Eastern art met and revered Mao Tse-tung, the revolutionary who had obliterated the ancient culture of China. Malraux used this round-the-world voyage to structure the narrative of the first volume of his enigmatic and strangely unrevealing *Antimemoirs* (1967).

When Malraux left the government with De Gaulle in 1969, after eleven years in office, he explained his decision by an imperfect analogy to Republican Spain: "Could you see me remaining with 'them' after the departure of the General? It is as if we had won the Spanish war and Negrin had asked me to become a colonel in the Guardia Civil"—though the Gaullist Malraux was much closer to the Guardia Civil than the Socialist Negrin.

Though freed from ministerial responsibility, Malraux continued to be active in both politics and art. In *Fallen Oaks* (1971) he created an idealized representation of his last meeting with De Gaulle in 1969 that is embarrassing in its fulsomeness and often absurd in its apotheosis. In 1972 Malraux was the subject of a series of French television programmes, "The Legend of the Century"; he tutored Nixon for his interview with Mao Tse-tung; and at the age of 71 he offered to found a school of guerrilla warfare in Bangladesh or to lead its army of independence against Pakistan—just as in 1919 Lawrence had offered to break Ibn Saud's Wahabi movement with ten tanks and Moslems from the Indian army. Malraux, who deserves the Nobel Prize more than any other writer but has not received it because of his political association with De Gaulle, published his earlier essays on Laclos, Goya and Saint-Just in *Le Triangle noir* (1970) and his ministerial speeches in *Oraisons funèbres* (1971), and he is now writing the second volume of *Antimemoirs*.

It is possible to interpret Malraux's life as a series of spectacular failures—in France, Indochina, Arabia and Spain—that paradoxically amount to a remarkable success. As he says of Mao's Long March, "it was a retreat, but its result was like a conquest." Malraux was not admitted to a *lycée*; his obscure early fantasies, lavishly printed in private editions, were almost completely unknown; he gambled away Clara's substantial inheritance; he was arrested for trying to remove Khmer sculpture from the Cambodian jungle and sentenced to prison; his journalistic and political career in support of the Young Annam League was ephemeral and totally ineffective; he was never in charge of propaganda for the Kuomintang in Canton; he was unable to free Dimitrov from a Nazi jail; he did not discover the lost city of the Queen of Sheba; and though he created and organized the Escadre España out of nothing, it was eventually defeated by German and Italian planes. Malraux was twice captured and imprisoned in the Second World War; he was accused of betraying the Left by joining the reactionary government of De Gaulle; he never realized his ministerial dream of an extensive system of French provincial Houses of Culture; and both of his marriages failed.

What is so impressive about Malraux's life, however, is that his sensitive idealism was never diminished by his failures and for fifty years, from Saigon to Bangladesh, he fought for just causes. He achieved a heroic record in two wars and brought moral standards to political activity, but he was more committed to art than to action, more to legend than to truth. When the opportunities for adventure coincided with his inclinations, he was capable of heroism; when they did not, he escaped into mythomania. Though his political accomplishments were limited, Malraux created in *L'Espoir* what Koestler calls "one of the greatest films ever made"; he published a number of ambitious and exciting books that revealed a new way of seeing art, both individually and contextually; and he wrote three first-rate novels. *Man's Fate, Man's Hope* and *The Walnut Trees of Altenburg,* whose heroes represent an idealized image of himself, defined the political conscience of his age.

SELECT BIBLIOGRAPHY

Blunt, Wilfred Scawen. *The Land War in Ireland.* London, 1912.
Blunt, Wilfred Scawen. *My Diaries, 1884-1914.* London, 1919-1920. 2 vols.
Blunt, Wilfred Scawen. *The Secret History of the English Occupation of Egypt.* London, 1907.
Curtis, Lewis. *Coercion and Conciliation in Ireland, 1880-1892.* Princeton, 1963.
Finch, Edith. *Wilfred Scawen Blunt, 1840-1922.* London, 1938.
Lytton, The Earl of. *Wilfred Scawen Blunt: A Memoir.* London, 1961.

Graham, R. B. Cunninghame. *Mogreb-el-Acksa.* London, 1898.
Graham, R. B. Cunninghame. *The Nail-and-Chainmakers: A Plea.* London Platform Series, no. 2. London, 1888. Pp. 101-110.
Shaw, G. B. *Captain Brassbound's Conversion.* London, 1899.
Tschiffely, A. F. *Don Roberto: The Life and Works of R. B. Cunninghame Graham.* London, 1937.
West, Herbert. *A Modern Conquistador: R. B. Cunninghame Graham, His Life and Works.* London, 1932.

Singleton-Gates, Peter and Maurice Girodias. *The Black Diaries of Sir Roger Casement.* New York, 1959.
Casement, Roger. *The Crime Against Europe.* ed. Herbert Mackey. Dublin, 1958.
Hyde, H. Montgomery, ed. *The Trial of Sir Roger Casement.* London, 1960.
Inglis, Brian. *Roger Casement.* London, 1973.
Meyers, Jeffrey. "Conrad and Roger Casement." *Conradiana,* 5 (1973), 64-69.
Shaw, G. B. *A Discarded Defence of Roger Casement.* London, 1922.

Carteggio D'Annunzio-Mussolini, 1919-1938. ed. Renzo De Felice e Emiliano Mariano. Verona, 1971.
D'Annunzio, Gabriele. *Prosa di ricerca, di lotta, di comando, di conquista . . .* Vol. I. Milano : Mondadori, 1954.
Gatti, Guglielmo. *Vita di Gabriele D'Annunzio.* Firenze, 1956.
Jullian, Philippe. *D'Annunzio.* London, 1972.
Meyers, Jeffrey. "Hero Who Built His Own Valhalla." *Daily Telegraph Magazine,* 5 September 1975, pp. 32-38.
Rhodes, Anthony. *D'Annunzio: The Poet as Superman.* London, 1959.

Lawrence, T. E. *Letters.* ed. David Garnett. London, 1964.

Lawrence, T. E. *Seven Pillars of Wisdom.* New York, 1935.

T. E. Lawrence to His Biographers Robert Graves and Liddell Hart. London, 1963.

Knightley, Phillip and Colin Simpson. *The Secret Lives of Lawrence of Arabia.* New York, 1970.

Lawrence, A. W., ed. *T. E. Lawrence By His Friends.* London, 1937.

Meyers, Jeffrey. *The Wounded Spirit: A Study of 'Seven Pillars of Wisdom'.* London, 1973.

Malraux, André. *Antimemoirs.* London, 1968.

Malraux, André. *Days of Hope* (1937). London, 1970.

Malraux, André. "Lawrence and the Demon of the Absolute." *Hudson Review,* 8 (1956), 519-532.

Flanner, Janet. "André Malraux." *Men and Monuments.* London, 1957. pp. 19-87.

Lacouture, Jean. *André Malraux.* New York, 1975.

Langlois, Walter. *Malraux and the Indochina Adventure.* London, 1966.

Malraux, Clara. *Memoirs.* London, 1967.

DATE DUE